Conducting the UNIX System Administrator Job Interview

IT Manager's Guide for UNIX System Administrator Job Interviews with UNIX Interview Questions

Adam Haeder

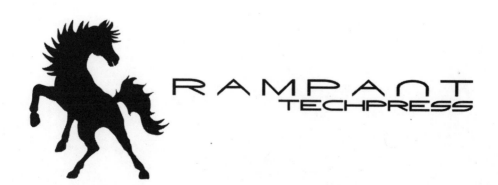

This book is dedicated to my immediate and extended family, for helping me keep my skills up by continuing to break their computers.

--- Adam Haeder

Conducting the UNIX System Administrator Job Interview

IT Manager's Guide for UNIX System Administrator Job Interviews with UNIX Interview Questions

By Adam Haeder

Copyright © 2004 by Rampant TechPress. All rights reserved.

Printed in the United States of America.

Published by Rampant TechPress, Kittrell, North Carolina, USA

IT Job Interview Series: Book #2

Series Editor: Don Burleson

Editors: Janet Burleson, John Lavender, Andy Liles, and Linda Webb

Production Editor: Teri Wade

Cover Design: Bryan Hoff

Printing History:

February 2004 for First Edition

Flame Warriors illustrations are copyright © by Mike Reed Illustrations Inc.

ISBN: 0-9744355-6-2

Library of Congress Control Number: 2004101843

Table of Contents

Using the Online Code Depot

Your purchase of this book provides you with complete access to the online code depot that contains the sample tests and answers.

All of the job questions in this book are located at the following URL:

rampant.cc/job_unix.htm

All of the sample tests and questions in this book will be available for download in a zip format, ready to use for your next interview.

If you need technical assistance in downloading or accessing the scripts, please contact Rampant TechPress at info@rampant.cc.

Get the Advanced Oracle Monitoring and Tuning Script Collection

The complete collection from Mike Ault, the world's best DBA.

Packed with 590 ready-to-use Oracle scripts, this is the definitive collection for every Oracle professional DBA.

It would take many years to develop these scripts from scratch, making this download the best value in the Oracle industry.

It's only $39.95 (less than 7 cents per script!)

To buy for immediate download, go to
www.rampant.cc/aultcode.htm

Conventions Used in this Book

It is critical for any technical publication to follow rigorous standards and employ consistent punctuation conventions to make the text easy to read.

However, this is not an easy task. Within UNIX there are many types of notations that can confuse a reader. Some UNIX utilities are always spelled in CAPITAL letters, while UNIX parameters and procedures have varying naming conventions in the documentation. It is also important to remember that all UNIX commands are case sensitive, and are always left in their original executable form, and never altered with italics or capitalization.

Hence, all Rampant TechPress books follow these conventions:

Parameters - A *lowercase italics font* will be used to identify all UNIX parameters. Exceptions to this rule are parameter arguments that are commonly capitalized; these will be left in ALL CAPS.

Variables – All program variables and arguments will also remain in *lowercase italics*.

Programs & Products – All products and programs that are known to the author are capitalized according to the vendor specifications (IBM, DBXray, etc). All names known by Rampant TechPress to be trademark names appear in this text as initial caps. References to UNIX are always made in uppercase.

Acknowledgements

This type of highly technical reference book requires the dedicated efforts of many people. Even though I am the author, my work ends when I deliver the content. After each chapter is delivered, several UNIX experts carefully review and correct the technical content. After the technical review, experienced copy editors polish the grammar and syntax. The finished work is then reviewed as page proofs and turned over to the production manager, who arranges the creation of the online code depot and manages the cover art, printing distribution, and warehousing.

In short, I played a small role in the development of this book, and I need to thank and acknowledge everyone who helped bring this book to fruition:

John Lavender, for the production management, including the coordination of the cover art, page proofing, printing, and distribution.

Linda Webb, for all of his efforts and assistance in getting this book published in a timely manner.

Teri Wade, for her help in the production of the page proofs.

Bryan Hoff, for his exceptional cover design and graphics.

Janet Burleson, for her assistance with the web site, and for creating the code depot and the online shopping cart for this book.

With sincerest thanks,

Adam Haeder

Preface

After interviewing hundreds of candidates for UNIX System Administrator related positions, it is obvious that it is getting harder to locate and retain qualified UNIX professionals. You must cull the best fit for the job from hundreds of résumés. Success depends upon knowing exactly which skills you need, and verifying that each candidate possesses acceptable levels of those skills.

That's where this book can help you. For both the new UNIX manager and the seasoned VP, the levels within the UNIX professional position will be explained to illustrate screening and interview techniques. Some common misconceptions will be clarified about the UNIX professional position and tips will be provided on how to interview a candidate.

Few IT managers, especially in smaller companies, have extensive formal training in interviewing and hiring techniques. Most interviewers' primary full-time responsibility will lie elsewhere. It is a fact that most IT managers do not even have a clear idea of the skills and personal characteristics their candidate should possess, much less an effective process for screening potential employees. Yet, nothing is more crucial to the success of the organization than doing everything possible to insure that the selected candidate is the best fit for the available position.

This book will provide effective techniques for finding committed employees who are able to function at a high level on the job. By eliminating guesswork, and rejecting the random hit-or-miss approach that is based on the instincts of the interviewer and little else, the employer can hire promising candidates with the confidence that the odds are stacked in his favor.

To help find, hire, and retain suitable UNIX professionals, background evaluation tips will be provided for identifying the best candidates. For the technical interview, sample technical questions and answers are also provided. A non-technical evaluation section is provided to help determine whether the candidate's personality is a good match for the organization allowing your chosen candidate to integrate seamlessly with your shop's particular culture.

Of course, there is no magic formula for determining if a candidate can perform properly, and no single screening test to ensure that you will properly evaluate a candidate's ability. However, if the employer and candidate are properly prepared, then filling the position successfully becomes much less chancy.

It is our hope that this book will be an indispensable tool for identifying, interviewing, and hiring top-notch UNIX professionals.

Evaluation

System Administrator Evaluation

UNIX has been around for a long time. From its roots in research institutions and higher education, to its present day place as the workhorse operating system of most major companies, UNIX has proven time and again that it has a place in most IT departments.

The rise of the Linux operating system has breathed new life into UNIX, making it more easily accessible to anyone interested in learning the operating system, as well as becoming the defacto standard for IT curriculums in most major colleges. The combination of price and performance that Linux affords is hard to beat when companies are examining the bottom line.

The consequence is a renewed interest in UNIX skills throughout the IT marketplace resulting in many more candidates with some UNIX background on their résumés. This has essentially created a two-tiered job market. Many top-rated universities teach UNIX as part of their undergraduate CS or IT curriculum and produce system administrators for career tracks in large corporations. At the same time, trade schools and community colleges produce thousands of IT and MIS graduates. No matter what the economic climate, large corporations actively recruit their entry-level talent for their mission-critical system administration roles from prestigious universities.

Preparing the UNIX System Administrator Job Offering

One of the points that we repeatedly make is that top-notch UNIX professionals are hard to find and well compensated, while mediocre UNIX professionals are easy to find and hire.

On the high end, UNIX system administrators with over 10 years' experience and graduate degrees typically command salaries ranging from $80,000 to $140,000 per year, depending on geographical location. For UNIX consultants with a broad exposure in mission-critical areas, the sky is the limit.

On the other end of the spectrum, we see overseas system administrator trainees who will work remotely from Bangalore, India for as little as $10/per hour, and beginners who are desperate for a chance to learn UNIX on your multi-million dollar production servers.

The first step in hiring a UNIX professional is determining the level of skill you require and preparing an incentive package. If your UNIX systems are mission-critical, then a seasoned system administrator is your safest choice. People with high Skill levels often require incentives to abandon their employers.

Preparing the Incentive Package

If you want a top-notch senior UNIX professional, you may be surprised to find them in short supply, even in a down job market. While every manager knows that salary alone cannot guarantee employee loyalty, there are a host of techniques used by IT management to attract and retain the top-notch UNIX professional.

UNIX Professionals like the latest hardware and software

In addition to a competitive salary, some of the techniques used to entice potential candidates include:

Flex time - Burnout can be a real problem among the system administrators who typically work evenings and holidays to maintain the computer systems. Many companies offer formal comp-time policies or institute a four-day work week, allowing four 10-hour days per week.

Telecommuting - Many UNIX professionals are allowed to work at home and only visit the office once per week for important face-to-face meetings.

Golden handcuffs - Because a high base salary does not always reduce attrition, many IT managers use yearly bonuses to retain employees. Golden handcuffs may take the form of a Management by Objective (MBO) structure, whereby the system administrator receives a substantial annual bonus for meeting management expectations. Some companies implement golden handcuffs by paying the employee a huge signing bonus (often up to $50,000) and requiring the employee to return the bonus if he or she leaves the company in less than three years. However, don't be surprised to find that some competing companies will reimburse the system administrator to repay a retention bonus.

Office perks - Since many senior UNIX professionals command salaries commensurate with those received by corporate Vice Presidents, some are offered private offices and company cars.

Fancy job titles - Because UNIX professionals command high salaries, many are given honorary job titles. These include "fellows" titles such as the Apple fellow, whereby the corporation grants special privileges to employees who have been granted fellow status. Other UNIX professional titles include Vice President of Systems Administration, Chief Technologist, and the new job title (used by Bill Gates), Chief Software Architect.

Specialized training – System administrators are commonly rewarded by being allowed to attend conferences and training classes. An entire industry is built around these large events. For example, cruises have become an extremely popular reward for the UNIX professional. The Geek Cruise Line is typical of this movement, offering technical conferences on hot topics in UNIX, Java, and Perl, combined with an ocean cruise. Companies pack these cruise ships with their UNIX professionals, sailing to exotic destinations in Alaska, Hawaii, and the Mediterranean.

Defining the Required Job Skills

A number of UNIX professionals mistakenly believe that their job is purely technical. In reality, the system administrator must be an "ace" of all IT functions. He or she has ultimate responsibility for overall system design, implementation, backup, and recovery. Excellent interpersonal skills and communicative abilities are required, as well as technical skills, for the system administrator's close involvement in all phases of project development.

Remember, knowledge of UNIX is not enough. An understanding of operating systems and computer-science theory is imperative as well. That is why employers like to hire UNIX system administrators who have a background in computer programming, information systems, or business administration.

It's critical to remember that certification tells employers only that the job candidate successfully passed a certification test on the technical aspects of UNIX. In the real world, UNIX certification is just one of many criteria used to evaluate a candidate. Other criteria include the following:

Excellent Communication Skills - The system administrator is the central technical guru for the shop. He or she must be able to explain system concepts clearly developers and programmers using the servers. In many shops, the system administrator is also a manager and is required to have excellent communication skills for participating in strategic planning and architectural reviews.

Formal Education – Many employers require system administrators to have a bachelor's degree in computer science or information systems. For advanced positions such as Senior UNIX System Administrator, many employers prefer a master's degree in computer science or a master's in business administration (MBA).

Real-World Experience - This requirement is the catch-22 for newbies who possess only a basic UNIX certification, such as Sun's Certified Solaris Administrator or RedHat's RHCE. A common complaint of people who have certifications but no job experience is that they cannot get experience without the certification, and they cannot get a job without experience. This is especially true in a tight job market.

Basic IT Skills

Because the UNIX professional is often called-upon to perform critical projects in the IT department, a broad background is often desirable. Much of this basic IT knowledge is taught in academic Computer Science and Information Technology programs. Non-UNIX job skills include:

System Analysis & Design – Many UNIX professionals must take an active role in the analysis and design of new systems. Hence, knowledge of CASE tools, entity-relation modeling and design techniques enhance the UNIX professional's scope of ability.

Physical Disk Storage – Understanding of disk hardware architecture, cache controllers, and disk load balancing are beneficial to any UNIX professional.

Data Security Principles – A thorough understanding of UNIX security, including role-based security, is essential, especially for US Government positions.

Backup and Recovery Techniques – Many backup and recovery methods involve third-party software (Veritas, Legato, ADSM), and the candidate should have real-world experience implementing backup and recovery methods.

Change Control Management – In many cases the UNIX professional is charged with the task of implementing change control and ensuring that changes to the production systems are properly coordinated. Knowledge of third-party change control tools, such as the UNIX Source Code Control System (SCCS), rcs, or cvs is beneficial.

Now that we understand the basic skills, let's talk about UNIX certification. The two most popular UNIX certifications are Sun Microsystems' Certified System Administrator for the Solaris Operating System, and RedHat's RedHat Certified Engineer (RHCE). These certification exams identify candidates who have mastered specific technical areas within UNIX system administration. However, as interviewers frequently discover, possession of a certification is no guarantee that a candidate has real world expertise.

UNIX Certified Professionals

Lured by the promise of big bucks, thousands of ordinary people have managed to complete "IT boot camps" that teach them how to pass the certification exams. From shoe salesmen to auto mechanics, people are getting certified without the appropriate IT background. So then, what is the value of a certification?

The Value of UNIX Certification

Considering that certification exams cost over $100 each and that some certifications require up to five exams, then factoring in the cost of books, classes, and other study materials, UNIX

---

certification is a sizable investment. However, the potential rewards can make that investment worthwhile.

Here's the catch - certification alone is not a guarantee that anyone will find employment in system administration. The certification is just one of the credentials valued by prospective employers.

Sun Microsystems offers three levels of certification:

- Sun Certified System Administrator
- Sun Certified Network Administrator
- Sun Certified Security Administrator

RedHat offers two certifications:

- RedHat Certified Engineer
- RedHat Certified Technician

While UNIX certification is not a complete measure of a person's skills, it does demonstrate a modicum of talent and provides a method for those with degrees in Computer Science or Business Administration to enter the UNIX job field.

For a UNIX professional candidate, in-depth knowledge in computer programming concepts is far more important than the ability to pass a vendor's exam. Employers are recognizing the pitfalls of hiring people based solely upon certification.

The code depot User ID = reader; Password = hunter

UNIX Professional Characteristics

While many IT shops have hundreds of technology workers, retention efforts are normally focused on system administrators whose knowledge of the company's systems is not easily transferred to replacements.

In many shops, system administrators typically serve many roles. In addition to traditional UNIX duties, the system administrator is often called upon to serve as a system architect, an informaticist (a functional IT professional who possesses an MS in computer science and is also trained in professional areas, such as medicine or accounting), a database administrator, or a programmer. These 'renaissance' IT gurus are in high demand, as they have the ability to not only fill multiple roles, but their widespread knowledge gives them a unique perspective when it comes to troubleshooting or system design.

The following attributes are signs of a top-notch UNIX professional:

Has earned at least one professional degree or certification - Possessing a degree such as MD, JD, MBA, MSEE, or CPA, in addition to a computer science undergraduate degree, makes an employee a valuable asset, one difficult to replace in the open job market.

Has graduated from a competitive university – System administrators must be self-starting and highly motivated to be effective, and this is often indicated by entrance to competitive universities with rigorous admission standards. These schools include most Ivy League schools, especially MIT, and universities with stellar reputations in Information Systems such as Purdue, the University of Texas, the University of California at Los Angeles, the University of San Diego, and the University of California at Berkeley.

Active in the IT community - Many good UNIX professionals participate in local user groups, present techniques, and publish in many of the UNIX-related periodicals.

Is recognized as an expert - A sure sign of a UNIX all-star is someone who gets in front of audiences by publishing a book, writing a magazine article, or appearing as a conference speaker.

Possesses irreplaceable knowledge of an institution's enterprise systems - If the employee serves in a mission-critical role, such as chief architect or senior system administrator, a vacuum in the IT department may be created by that employee's departure.

Sample Job Sheet for a UNIX System Administrator

Applicants for any system administrator job are expected to meet all the requirements in mission-critical areas, including education, experience, certification, writing credits, personal characteristics, and legal standing. Here is an example job requirement sheet for the position of System Administrator from an actual corporation:

Sample System Administrator Job Sheet

These are the minimum job requirements for the position of Senior System Administrator. The HR department will pre-screen all candidates for the following job skills and experience.

Education

Persons with Masters Degrees, Doctoral degrees and Ivy League graduates are desired. At a minimum, the candidate is expected to possess a four-year degree from a fully-accredited university in a discipline such as Computer Science, Software Engineering, BA or MBA in Information Systems (from an AACSB accredited university), or Engineering (electrical, mechanical, or chemical).

Work Experience

The system administrator candidate is required to have a minimum of five years of full-time, progressive experience in UNIX system administration and management.

Certification

The system administrator candidate must have earned an IT certification at some time in the last five years.

Publishing and Research

The candidate should show demonstrable interest in publishing systems research as evidenced by participating in user groups and publishing of articles, books and columns. These include:

- Books. UNIX technical books or any other recognized academic publication company.

- Articles for academic journals. For example, the Journal of the IEEE and the Journal of Information Systems.

- Conference papers. Writing papers and presenting at conferences such as LISA and LinuxWorld.

- Articles in trade publications. Writing an article for a trade publication such as SysAdmin Magazine, Network Magazine, or Linux Journal.

Personal Integrity

This position requires securing mission-critical applications and accessing confidential data. All candidates are required to sign a waiver to disclose personal information.

The system administrator candidate must have no history of acts of moral turpitude, drug use, dishonesty, lying, cheating, or theft.

USA Citizenship

We are unable to sponsor H1-B foreign consultants. Therefore, candidates must provide proof of US citizenship.

Additional Specialized Skills

The following specialized skills are desired:

- Masters or Doctorate degree from a major university
- An active US Secret, Top secret or Q-level security clearance
- SAP, Oracle, or DB2 DBA experience

As we can see, UNIX system administrator positions have requirements that vary widely, and it is up to the IT manager to choose those qualities that best suit the position.

Conclusion

This chapter has been concerned with identifying the job requirements and preparing an incentive package. Next, let's take a look at how to evaluate the UNIX professional for specific job skills.

Qualities of the System Administrator

The evaluation of the résumé is a critical part of the selection process. In a tight job market, it is not uncommon to receive hundreds of résumés, and it is the job of the HR or IT manager to fairly and efficiently pre-screen applicants and only forward qualified individuals to the hiring manager for a detailed interview. Let's start by looking at techniques for evaluating the job history of a UNIX professional.

A good UNIX programmer will demonstrate persistence!

Evaluating Employment History

Evaluation of a job candidate's work history is the single most critical factor in résumé screening. Candidates without significant work history may spend an undue amount of time learning their jobs, while a more expensive, experienced candidate may be a better overall value for the hiring company.

Not all UNIX experience is equal. Many demanding IT shops provide excellent training and experience, while others provide only glancing exposure to system administration.

When evaluating work experience, the following factors need to be considered:

Job role – System administrator candidates who have had positions of responsibility within their organization are often more qualified than those candidates for whom the UNIX skills were a part-time duty.

Employer-sponsored system administration education - Many large corporations require yearly training for all IT employees, and on-the-job education is a clear indicator of the employer's quality. Employer-sponsored, yearly training and participation in user groups and conferences are indications of a good background for a UNIX system administrator.

Fraudulent Work History

In the soft market of the early twenty-first century, it is not uncommon for a desperate job applicant to forge a work history with a defunct dot-com. The desperate applicant hopes that this fraud will not be detected. This phenomenon presents the IT manager with a unique challenge in verifying employment history with a company that no longer exists or contacting job references who cannot speak English.

In many cases, the HR staff strongly discounts résumés where the employment and educational history cannot be completely verified. Many departments, frustrated with confirming overseas employment histories, never forward these types of résumés to the IT manager.

Evaluating Personal Integrity

It is always a good idea to perform a background check, which is easily obtained via national services. Many companies require that a candidate not have any criminal convictions, except minor traffic violations. In some cases, a routine background check can reveal arrests and acts of moral turpitude.

A system administrator's ongoing responsibilities often include securing mission-critical applications and confidential data. Therefore, some companies require that all applicants for senior system administrator positions be expected to demonstrate the highest degree of personal and moral integrity.

In addition, acts of moral turpitude, such as a history of drug use, dishonesty, lying, cheating, or theft may be grounds for immediate rejection. In some companies, all applicants are expected to sign a waiver to disclose personal information and are asked to submit to a polygraph exam.

Evaluating Academic History

While formal education is not always a predictor of success at a system administrator job, there can be no doubt that job candidates with advanced degrees from respected universities possess both the high intelligence and persistence needed in a top-notch UNIX professional.

The Quality of Education

When evaluating the educational background of job candidates, it is important to remember that not all colleges are created equal.

Many IT managers tend to select candidates from top tier colleges and universities because they rely on the universities to do the prescreening for them.

For example, an IT professional who has been able to enroll in a top tier university clearly demonstrates high achievement, high intelligence, and a very strong work ethic. At the other end of the spectrum, there are many IT candidates who have attended vocational schools, night schools, and non-accredited universities to receive bachelor's degrees in nontraditional study areas. In many cases, these IT professionals lack the necessary technical and communicational skills required to succeed in the IT industry.

The type of degree is also a factor in the suitability of the IT candidate. For example, an ABS or MS in Computer Science generally requires the IT job candidate to have a very strong theoretical background in mathematics and physics. Those with formal degrees in computer science tend to gravitate toward software engineering and software development fields that require in-depth knowledge about lower-level components in computer systems.

On the other hand, we see BS and MBA degrees in Information Systems. Those degrees offered by accredited business colleges (accredited by the American Assembly of Collegiate Business Schools, AACBS) tend to strike a balance between IT programming skills and business skills. The information systems degree candidate will have a background in systems analysis and design, as well as familiarity with functional program development for specific business processes.

Unlike computer science majors, information systems majors will have a background in accounting, finance, marketing, economics, and other areas of business administration that equip them to solve business problems.

Many IT shops save time by letting universities pre-screen system administrator candidates. For example, MIT carefully screens grades and achievement, and this pre-screening by the university allows companies to choose computer science professionals with increased confidence in the candidate's required skills.

The type of job to be filled may determine the academic history required. For example, a system administrator for a small IT shop may not require a four-year degree, while a Senior System Architect for a large corporation may need a Master's degree from a respected university.

Note: This section is based upon the author's experience in evaluating UNIX professionals and the HR policies of large IT shops. This section is in no way meant to discredit those job applicants without the benefit of a college education.

Rating College Education

Many shops have an HR professional evaluate education, while other IT managers take it upon themselves to evaluate the quality of the system administrator candidate's formal education. Fortunately, sources for rating colleges and universities can be found online. Many large corporations require that the job candidate's degree must be from a university possessing a first-tier or second-tier rating by US News & World Report's "America's Best Colleges" or degrees from exceptional universities (as listed in the Gourman Report).

Some computer professionals are insecure about their vocabulary

Of course, not all UNIX jobs require a college degree. For lower-level system administrator jobs, the formal academic requirements are less challenging, but the lead system administrator for a large corporation must possess high intelligence, superb communications skills, and the drive and persistence that is most commonly associated with someone who has taken the time to invest in a quality education.

College Major and System Administrator Job Suitability

There is a great deal of debate about what academic majors, if any, are the best indicators of success in a system administrator position. However, it is well documented that different majors attract students with varying abilities. The following list describes some indicators used in large corporations for assessing the relative value of different college majors:

Engineers - Engineers tend to make great IT professionals, especially those with degrees in Electrical Engineering (EE). An engineering curriculum teaches logical thinking and data structure theory that makes it easy for the engineer to learn UNIX and system administration quickly. However, while engineers have unimpeachable technical skills, their oral and written communication skills are often lacking. Therefore, IT managers should pay careful attention to communication skills when interviewing applicants with engineering degrees.

Business Majors - Business majors make excellent system analysts because of their training in finance, accounting, marketing, and other business processes. Many business schools also require matriculated students to take several courses in Information Technology. Not all college business schools are equal, though. When screening a job applicant with a business major, time should be taken to insure that the degree is from a business school accredited by the American Assembly of Collegiate Business Schools (AACSB). There are many fly-by-night business schools, and their depth of training may be vastly different.

Computer Science Majors - Computer scientists typically receive four years of extensive technical training, and are ideal candidates for system administration jobs requiring in-depth technical ability. However, like the engineers, many computer scientists have sub-standard communications skills.

Music Majors - For many years, IBM recruited from the ranks of college musicians because hiring managers found that musicians possessed an ability in logical thinking that made them ideal candidates for IT skill training.

Math Majors - Math majors tend to possess excellent logical thinking skills and often possess a background in computer science. Like many quantitative majors, social and communications skills may be a concern.

Education Majors - Evaluation of education majors is extremely difficult because of the wide variation in quality between universities. Nationally, GRE test rankings by academic major show that education majors consistently rank in the lowest 25% of knowledge. Any applicant with an education major should be carefully screened for technical skills, and the college ranking checked in US News & World Report's "America's Best Colleges".

International Degrees

A huge variation in quality exists among international degrees. Therefore, candidates with international degrees should be carefully checked in the "Gourman Report" of International Colleges and Universities.

Some sub-standard overseas colleges have no entrance requirements and require little effort from the student. There has also been a rash of résumé falsifications of college degrees from overseas colleges. The fraudulent applicant is often relying upon the human resource department's inability to successfully contact the overseas school to verify the applicant's degree.

In sum, international degrees should be carefully evaluated. It is recommended that, where appropriate, foreign language professionals be hired to write the letters to request verification of the graduate's attendance, and to obtain and translate the college transcript.

Advanced Degrees and System Administrator Professionals

Approximately 30% of system administrators for large corporations possess an advanced degree (Masters or Doctorate).

While an advanced degree shows dedication to a professional position, the quality of the degree is of paramount concern.

A higher ranking should be given to an on-site master's degree from a respected university than to a night school or "non-traditional" graduate school. These non-traditional schools often have far lower acceptance standards for students and are far less academically demanding than the top US graduate programs.

The New Graduate

Regardless of the educational experience of the graduate, there will likely be little in his/her background that will prepare him/her for the real-world business environment. Computer curricula tend to emphasize theoretical issues of interest to academicians that may have little direct bearing on the needs of your shop.

The recent graduate may have grandiose visions of designing and maintaining whole software systems. They may be very adept at writing code from scratch, but the fresh graduate will rarely be called upon to do this.

New College graduates are sometimes immature.

Instead, your company will need someone who can work within the existing software system without crashing and burning the edifice down. The paramount skill here is the ability to read OPC (Other People's Code). The candidate with the ability to slog through existing code and understand it is the candidate who will be able to add data and make changes in your production system without bringing operations to a grinding halt.

Moreover, the work that the new employee does on the software system will doubtless be modified and altered by others in the future, as new needs develop and hidden problem areas emerge. For this reason, a candidate who is able to show the technical interviewer that he has excellent documentation skills and habits can be a tremendous asset to the company over someone who is not accustomed to submitting work that must be accessible to others. Several of the questions in Chapter 5 are useful for gauging these traits.

Personality of the System Administrator

What is more important to managers, technical knowledge or personality? Many times, managers concentrate too much on technical skill, and a candidate's personality is overlooked.

In almost every core IT job function mentioned above, the system administrator's work is made up of interacting with vendors, users, developers, and managers. With that in mind, the following professional personality traits are, or ought to be, embodied by the successful system administrator.

Some UNIX programmers have split personalities.

These traits are important for people in almost any profession, but they are particularly important for system administrators. Let it be said of the successful system administrator that he or she is self-confident, curious, tenacious, polite, motivated, and a stickler for details.

Self-confidence

System administrators that lack self-confidence, ask the manager's opinion on every decision no matter how large or small, and show no initiative, are not all-star material. This indecision may be acceptable for a junior system administrator working under the supervision of a senior administrator, but the individual must learn to depend on his or her own judgment for important decisions.

In interviews, questions must be asked about problems encountered and how the applicant would resolve the problems. Answers provided should reflect self-confidence.

A Curious Nature

Curiosity is a core trait of the system administrator because the systems are constantly changing, and those changes are not always documented. A system administrator who is not curious is passive and reactive, while a curious one is proactive.

Some UNIX programmers don't take initiative.

The curious system administrator invests personal money to stay current. In interviews with potential hires, questions should be asked about the books and subscriptions the candidate relies upon. Needless to say, answers indicating sole reliance on "the documentation set" are not an indication of professional curiosity.

Because curiosity is a requirement for a good system administrator, another set of interview questions should involve the UNIX data dictionary and the constant flow of new utilities and packages provided by the different UNIX vendors.

A Tenacious Disposition

Like most disciplines in the IT industry, bulldog-like tenacity is required for troubleshooting as a system administrator. The

---

candidate should enjoy knuckling down on a problem and not giving up until an answer is found.

In many online forums, thousands of questions have been posted by UNIX professionals out in the field. Many times, the questions are about things that would have been solved if the system administrator had been tenacious and curious instead of giving up.

Polite Manners

A system administrator works closely with other people. Therefore, tact is required when dealing with developers, managers, and users.

UNIX programmers have a reputation for poor manners!

But, here's a fact of system administration life: project managers, developers, and users will bring forth unreasonable requests and impossible deadlines. Interpersonal skills must be cultivated by the system administrator to respond to such requests without burning bridges. Ill will is fostered outside the IT department by a rude administrator. The system administrator must be extra polite, beginning in the job interview.

Self-Motivating

Employers value self-starting employees who require little supervision. Twice as much self-motivation is expected from the system administrator than other IT professionals, primarily because the administrator must often take charge of critical system-related projects. In addition, successful system administrators prevent fires before they start, and smart administrators know what things can cause trouble if they are ignored.

Motivation is a major factor in successful UNIX programming.

Detail Orientation

Being detail-oriented is perhaps the most important trait for a system administrator. System administrators are often described as having an "anal" personality, after Sigmund Freud's theory of anal-retentive personalities. A good UNIX professional should not have to be told to crosscheck details or to document quirks observed during an installation. A detail-oriented person is early for an appointment and brings a PDA or calendar to an interview. Questions asked by the detail-oriented person are reflections of the research conducted about the potential new employer.

Attention to Detail is critical for UNIX debugging.

Conclusion

This chapter has been concerned with the specific criteria for evaluating work and academic history. Next, let's look at the roles of UNIX system professionals and get more insights into the characteristics of a successful system administrator.

Any UNIX programmer who is fluent in Klingon may have a personality disorder.

Roles for the System Administrator

A good system administrator candidate is able to articulate a solid knowledge of techniques in all areas of UNIX, including installation, configuration management, system security, monitoring and tuning, backup and recovery strategies, and troubleshooting. In addition, a successful system administrator in any organization must also possess above average communication skills.

Nit-picky UNIX programmers document everything!

System Administrator Job Roles

The job of system administrator means many things to many people. What the new administrator does is determined by the size of the employer. In a small shop, the system administrator's duties are much broader than in a corporation with teams of administrators dedicated to specific projects.

Is the employer doing development? Is it utilizing a third party package? The functions of the system administrator position are also determined by the answers to those questions. The interviewee and the interviewer must be prepared to discuss and understand what is expected of the administrator and the role of the individual within the company hierarchy.

Here are some common job duties for the system administrator:

User Management - The system administrator is responsible for enrolling users and maintaining system security.

Storage Management - Allocation of system storage and plans for future storage requirements for the systems are duties of the system administrator. Archived data must be maintained on appropriate storage devices.

Disaster Recovery - A key duty is to back up and restore all systems or communicate backup requirements to the storage management team.

Hardware Management - Installation and upgrades to the production servers and application tools are performed by the system administrator.

End-user Liaison - In contacting vendors for technical support, the system administrator becomes the official company representative and contact point. Compliance with vendor license agreements is also insured by the system administrator.

To sum it up, a full-charge system administrator candidate is knowledgeable in installation, configuration management, system security, monitoring and tuning techniques, backup and recovery strategies, vendor relations, and of course, the day-to-day honor of chief troubleshooter.

Let's drill-down and review the basic knowledge areas for the system administrator candidate.

Installation

Because each platform is different, the successful system administrator stays current regarding installation and updates on the platform against which a system is running. Staying current isn't easy. Incorrect updates performed on production machines can result in big trouble.

In interviews for a system administrator position, questions about installing and upgrading UNIX systems are to be expected. The candidate should be prepared to discuss his or her platform of choice and any modifications to the standard installation that they employ.

Configuration Management

A successful system administrator is able to manage configuration, including capacity planning, logical volume management and user and group administration.

System Security

Having a clear understanding of UNIX security options is fundamental to the system administrator skill set.

Monitoring and Tuning

Part of the system administrator's daily routine is monitoring and tuning the systems and associated applications. The system administrator's knowledge base must include detailed understanding of the operating system. A top system administrator is able to maximize the benefits of the operating system, and ensure that it always performs at the highest level.

Backup and Recovery Strategies

A system administrator candidate's understanding of UNIX backup and recovery options may be discovered by questions covering the import and export utilities, use of cold and hot backups, and recovery scenarios involving different flavors of UNIX.

Troubleshooting

The flair for troubleshooting is a characteristic that is not common to all people. The art of troubleshooting requires an analytical approach, where the problem is laid out in discrete parts, and each is attacked in a methodical fashion until the problem can be resolved.

A good UNIX programmer is always available!

Troubleshooting sometimes requires the system administrator to admit he or she does not know something and must have the wherewithal to look for the answer. In responding to questions about troubleshooting, the candidate should be prepared to discuss real-life experiences. The best examples are those illustrating a lot of thought and multiple troubleshooting steps.

Communication Skills

Great technical skills are needed by the system administrator, but technical knowledge alone does not guarantee job success. As mentioned earlier, a system administrator needs to be polite when dealing with fellow administrators, managers, vendors, and end users. Because a significant percentage of the system administrator's work requires interacting with others on multiple levels, they must be able to speak, think, and write clearly and concisely. A system administrator should strive to set the standard for quality oral and written communication skills.

An inventory of a system administrator's communication skills starts with the professional résumé. The résumé should be easy to read and reflect the candidate's publishing and speaking credits. Whether the candidate was a keynote speaker at a national conference or merely presented a topic at a local user group, those experiences document the candidate's communication skills.

The interviewer should bring questions about job experiences that required the candidate to write documentation or procedures. It should be assumed that candidates with an advanced degree, such as a Masters' or PhD, have well-developed writing skills, or they would not have reached that level of education. Candidates are encouraged to bring to the interview their dissertations or other writing samples.

A successful candidate absolutely must possess strong verbal communication skills. The ability to listen is just as important as the ability to speak clearly. The professional system administrator's daily routine will include listening to complaints and requests, processing that information, and providing responses and instructions.

Conclusion

In sum, the system administrator must have a well-rounded skill set, and not just technical skills. Next, let's explore screening techniques for system administrators and examine techniques and tools for verifying technical skill.

You can always tell a successful UNIX programmer.

Initial Screening

Preparation

Significant amounts of money and resources can be saved by thorough preparation and attention to detail during the screening process. Preparation can also prevent potentially disastrous problems from ever occurring. Filling vacant positions is expensive, and a careful approach during the initial screening can reap tremendous dividends over time.

Be sure to screen for mental health issues!

In the opinion of many IT managers, an effective system administrator should have plenty of significant real-world experience to supplement technical knowledge. In many large corporations, the system administrator is a respected technical guru who participates in all phases of system development, from the initial system analysis to the final physical implementation. Hence, the system administrator generally has significant experience in development and systems analysis.

Troubleshooting skills are essential for the UNIX professional

The High Cost of Attrition and Hiring Overhead

The IT industry suffers from one of the highest attrition rates of all professional job categories. This is due, in part, to the dynamic nature of technology, where a job candidate may find himself grossly underpaid and decide to market his skills within a relatively short period of time. The high attrition rate is also due to the lack of challenge within many IT shops that can occur after the job candidate has been successful in their work.

For example, an IT job candidate might enter a shop that needs a great deal of work, only to stabilize the environment to the point where they tend to be bored most of the time. The IT manager must try to distinguish between the "job hopper" and the individual who is changing jobs solely because of a personal need for more challenging work.

The cost of hiring varies by position and by geographic location, but is rarely less than $10,000 per employee. Filling higher end positions, such as senior network administrator or database administrator, can often exceed $50,000, as specialized headhunters are required in order to locate the candidate, and these headhunters commonly charge up to 50 percent of the candidate's first year wages for a successful placement. There are also the fixed costs of performing background checks and credit checks, as well as HR overhead incurred in checking the individual's transcripts and other resume information.

Choosing Viable Candidates

While reviewing hundreds of applications for a single job, the IT manager must quickly weed-out "posers" and job candidates who do not know their own limitations. To be efficient, the IT manager must quickly drill-down and identify the best three candidates to invite for an in-depth technical interview by an experienced system administrator. Shops that do not have a current system administrator generally hire an outside consultant for this task.

UNIX consultants are commonly asked to help companies find the best system administrator for a permanent position. Later on, we show some of the questions used when evaluating candidates for corporate clients.

"Yes, I know Java, UNIX and two other computer words."

Dealing with IT Headhunters

When seeking a top-level IT position such as senior database administrator, database architect, or chief of network security, it is not uncommon to employ IT headhunters. These IT headhunters can charge up to 50 percent of the IT job's base salary in return for a successful placement.

However, the aggressive nature of the IT headhunters often does a disservice to the IT candidate, and puts the IT manager in a tenuous position. For example, it is not uncommon for the IT manager to receive Résumés from two different sources for the same candidate, each represented by different head hunting firms. In cases like this, it is prudent to immediately remove that candidate from the prospective pool, in order to avoid the inevitable feuding between the competing headhunter firms.

When dealing with headhunters, it's also important to get a guarantee that the IT employee will remain in the shop for a period of at least one year and to amortize the payments to the headhunter over that period. Those IT managers who fail to do this may find themselves spending up to $50,000 for a job candidate who quits within ninety days because they are not satisfied with their new job.

It's also important to remember to negotiate the rate with the headhunters. While they may typically command anywhere between 25 and 50 percent of the IT employee's first year gross wages, these terms can indeed be negotiated prior to extending an offer to the IT candidate. In many cases, this works to the disadvantage of the IT candidate, especially when the headhunter refuses to negotiate the terms, thereby making another candidate more financially suitable for the position.

General Evaluation Criteria

Remember, all system administrators are not created equal. They range from the UNIX System BS (UNIX System Baby Sitter) level to a fully skilled, fire-breathing hacker with extensive credentials. What level of system administrator does the company require? Consider what happens if a high-end administrator is employed in a position that requires only monitoring and backing up of a handful of servers. He will soon grow bored and find more challenging work elsewhere. On the other hand, hiring a UNIX System BS for a slot that requires tenacity, drive, initiative, and top-shelf troubleshooting skills is begging for disappointment.

Not all UNIX programmers have equal intelligence.

It is not easy to match the right candidate for a given job. Given the choice between someone who could re-write a UNIX kernel from scratch (but lacked certain personality skills) and a technically inexperienced system administrator who demonstrates the personality traits mentioned above, the less experienced candidate is frequently the best choice.

The typical UNIX System Baby Sitter usually has a good-looking résumé that is full of projects and jobs involving UNIX. However, the interviewer must subtract points if that work involved third-party applications that were pre-installed and the candidate's main duties were monitoring. When the candidate can't answer in-depth questions concerning the UNIX operating system, the person is a UNIX System BS rather than qualified candidate.

Networking skills may be desirable for a UNIX programmer.

A rule of thumb for hiring system administrators is to avoid hiring an overqualified person who won't be happy in a job with minimal responsibilities. In a small shop that utilizes out-of-the-box configurations and relies mostly on vendors for support, a UNIX System BS should be hired who can jump into gear whenever an obvious problem arises.

On the other hand, if a full-charge system administrator is needed, a newbie should not be hired, unless the newbie clearly demonstrates the motivation for high-end learning and the desire to become a full-fledged UNIX system administrator.

Gleaning Demographics from the Candidate

With the strict privacy laws in the United States, the IT manager must be careful never to ask any questions that are inappropriate or illegal. For example, asking the marital status, the number and age of the children, or the age of the applicant himself may make the IT manager vulnerable to age and sex discrimination lawsuits. Hence, the savvy IT manager learns to ask "safe" questions that still reveal the information, while protecting the manager and company from lawsuits.

Don't wind-up in court over an illegal interview question!

While the IT manager certainly does not want to discriminate against the job applicant, the demographical aspects of the job applicant nevertheless factor strongly into the hiring decision. For example, the female job applicant that has three children under five years of age may not be appropriate for an IT position that requires long hours on evenings and weekends.

Elderly UNIX programmers can add spice to the workplace!

Another example is age. If the IT manager works for a company that guarantees retirement where age plus years of service equals 70, then hiring a 60-year-old candidate would expose the company to paying that candidate a lifetime pension for only a few years of service.

Other important demographical information in our highly mobile society is the depth of connection the IT candidate has to the community. Those IT candidates who do not have extended family, close relatives, and long-term relationships in the community may be tempted to leave the position in order to seek more lucrative opportunities in other geographical areas.

Given that this information is critical to the hiring decision and at the same time inappropriate to ask directly, the savvy IT manager may ask somewhat ambiguous questions in order to get this information. For example, the manager may ask "What do you do to relax"? This open-ended question will often prompt the candidate to talk about activities they engage in with their families and with the community.

Generally, the selection of a system administrator can be accomplished through the following phases:

- Initial screening of résumés by HR department (keyword scan)

- Non-technical screening by IT manager (telephone interview)

- In-depth technical assessment by a senior system administrator or equivalent consultant

- On-site interview (check demeanor, personality, and attitude)

- Background check (verify employment, education, certification)

- Written job offer

Résumé Evaluation

As mentioned, it is not uncommon to receive hundreds of résumés for a particular system administration job. The goal of the IT manager (or HR department) is to filter through this mountain of résumés and identify the most-qualified candidates for the job interview.

The HR department typically performs a quick filtering through a large stack of résumés in order to narrow the candidates down to a select few, which are in turn presented to the IT manager.

Some résumés may contain anomalies that can reduce the time required for screening. These résumé anomalies are known as "red flags", and indicate that the job candidate might not be appropriate for the IT position. These indicators can quickly weed out dozens of candidates, eliminating the need for a more detailed analysis of the resume, saving company resources.

Resume Red Flags

There are several important things to look at when scanning a stack of résumés. The following are a short list that is used by many IT managers:

Unconventional resume formatting and font - Occasionally you may see a nice resume that is done in a professional font, with elaborate graphics, sometimes even including photographs and illustrations. In extreme cases, résumés have been known to arrive printed on pink paper scented with expensive perfumes.

Too much information in the resume - Another red flag for the IT professional is a resume that tends to specify a great deal of non-technical information. For example, the job candidate may go into great detail about their love of certain sports, hobbies, or religious and social activities. In many cases, these résumés indicate an individual for whom the IT profession is not a great priority.

Puffing insignificant achievements - It is not uncommon for low end IT positions to attract job candidates who will exaggerate the importance of trivial training. For example, an IT job candidate may proudly list on his resume that he attended classes on how to use Windows e-mail in the work environment. Of course, trivia within an otherwise nice resume too often indicates a lack of real technical skill, and the job candidate may be making an effort to obfuscate that fact by simply listing anything that they can think of.

Gaps in employment time - It's important to understand that the technically competent IT professional is always in demand and rarely has any kind of gaps in their employment history. Sometimes, IT professionals misrepresent their work chronology in their résumés. For example, if they are laid off and are job seeking for 90 days, they may not list that ninety-day gap of unemployment in order to make themselves seem more attractive. Of course, the start and end dates of each term of employment must be carefully checked by the HR department, and any false indication of this should be grounds for immediate removal from the candidate pool.

Poor grammar and sentence structure - Because the IT industry tends to focus more on technical than verbal skills, you may often find candidates with exceptional technical skills but whose poor writing ability is clearly apparent on their résumés. Short, choppy sentences, incorrect use of verbs, and misspellings can often give you a very good idea of the candidate's ability to communicate effectively via e-mail. Remember, the resume is a carefully crafted and reviewed document. If you find errors in this, you're likely to hire a candidate who lacks adequate written communicative skills.

Short employment periods - Within the IT industry, it is very rare to be dismissed from a position in less than six months. Even the incompetent IT worker is generally given 90 days before they're put on probation and another 90 days before they are dismissed from the job. Hence, an immediate red flag would be any IT employee whose resume indicates that they've worked with an employer for less than 6 elapsed months.

"Yes, I was an NCAA Basketball All-star"
Some job candidates may lie!

Evaluating Training

Scanning résumés involves two factors: evaluation of work history and academic qualifications. Here are some criteria that have been used by major corporations for résumé screening.

System administrator job candidates used to have only two sources for UNIX knowledge: experience and/or vendor training classes. Experience speaks for itself and can be judged as to depth and level of experience. However, any training is only as good as what the candidate puts into the training. In other words, the candidate could either gain much or comparatively little from the experience of vendor training, depending on whether they took their "will to learn" and curiosity with them to class.

As we have noted, RHCE certification (offered by RedHat) is one benchmark of a modicum of competence. The exams test the candidate's knowledge in all areas of the professional skill set.

In order to pass, a candidate will in almost all cases need to have had actual experience as a UNIX professional and will need to have knowledge from multiple system administration references. While obtaining a certification from this exam is no absolute guarantee that a candidate is fully qualified, it can be used as an acid test to separate the wheat from the chaff.

"I've been programming in UNIX for 35 years."

Telephone Screening

After reviewing the available résumés, you will be in a position to select a pool of candidates for further telephone screening. The telephone interview is a useful tool for weeding those candidates whose actual qualities may not quite match their glowing résumés, saving considerable time and expense over on-site interviews.

The interview may be either unscheduled or prearranged. In both cases, the candidate will be less prepared than for the more formal on-site interview, and it can quickly become apparent that a candidate is inappropriate to fill the position.

The telephone is your best tool for pre-screening technical skills.

The unscheduled telephone screening is an opportunity to discover how well the candidate thinks on his feet, and provides insight into his unrehearsed thoughts and feelings. It can also indicate how well the candidate is organized, since the person who has to repeatedly search for basic necessary materials and documents at home is unlikely to demonstrate superior efficiency in the work environment.

The interviewer should cover all pertinent areas, with the goal of confirming the qualifications present in the resume. The candidate should be well-informed about those topics which the resume indicates are areas of proficiency.

The telephone interview will also reveal a great deal about non-technical qualifications. Is the candidate personable and articulate? How well do they listen?

The information and impressions gathered from the telephone screening will enable the IT manager to confidently select the best-qualified candidates for an in-depth technical interview.

Technical Pre-Testing

The job interview questions in this text are deliberately intended to be presented orally. While these questions often indicate a high degree of experience and skill with a specific technology, many IT managers will require the job candidate to take an in-depth technical examination.

The technical examination may be given over the internet, using job testing sites such as Brain Bench, or they may be paper and pencil tests administered to the candidate before the start of a detailed job interview.

There are important legal ramifications for the use of these testing methods. Many job candidates who are not selected for an important position may challenge both the scope and validity of the test itself. These challenges have been applied even to nationally-known aptitude tests such as the SAT and LSAT exams; IT exams and language tests, such as C++, may be especially prone to challenge by the disgruntled IT professional.

While it is important to do a complete check of all the technical abilities of the IT candidate, it is very important for the IT manager never to cite the failure of one of these exams as the reason for removal from the applicant pool. This is a common technique used by IT managers when they find a particular candidate's knowledge of the field to be insufficient.

For example, in a highly competitive IT vacancy, very small things may wind up making the difference. In any case, when rejecting a candidate, the IT manager should generally cite something intangible, such as the job skills do not completely meet the requirements of the position, or a more nebulous answer, such as the candidate's interpersonal skills will not mesh with the team environment. Remember, specific citation of failure of any tangible IT testing metric may open your company to challenges and lawsuits.

Developing Questions for Interviews

Interview questions should be diligently researched and the expected answers listed prior to the interview. Where open-ended questions are used, the interviewer should have the level of knowledge required to judge the correctness of the answers given by the candidate.

You cannot always identify drug users

- The questions should be broken into categories and each should be assigned a point value based on either a scale, such as from 0-5 or according to difficulty. Technically competent personnel should review interview questions for accuracy and applicability.

- At the conclusion of the interview, evaluation of technical ability should be based on the results from these points.

In addition, "open-ended" questions should be included, such as "Describe the most challenging problem you have solved to date", or "Name one item that you have developed that you are most proud of". These open-ended questions are designed to allow the job candidate to articulate and demonstrate their communications skills.

The IT Candidate's Demeanor

During the face-to-face interview, the IT manager can glean a great deal about the personality of the individual simply by observing his/her body language and listening to the candidate speak. In many cases, the IT manager may base the assessment of the interview candidate on non-technical criteria, especially the behavior of the candidate when asked pointed questions. Some of these demeanor factors include:

Eye Contact

IT candidates who are unwilling or unable to maintain eye contact with the interviewer may not possess the interpersonal skills required to effectively communicate with end-users and co-workers.

Fidgeting

IT candidates who are experiencing high anxiety during an interview may cross and uncross their legs, sit uncomfortably, or twiddle their hair while speaking with the IT manager. These involuntary signs of discomfort may indicate that the candidate does not function well in the stressful environment of a busy IT shop.

Diction

For those IT positions that require exceptional communicative skills, such as working with the end-user community, you can get a very good idea of the abilities of the job candidates simply by listening to their responses. For example, careful IT professionals may demonstrate the "lawyer's pause" before answering the question. This pause, of about two seconds, often indicates that the job candidate is thinking carefully and formulating his response before speaking.

Job candidates who formulate their answers carefully can be especially useful in those positions where the risk of damage from impulsive verbal statements, without considering the consequences of the statement, is high. You can also assess how articulate the job candidate is by the use of filler words such as "you know", inappropriate pauses, poor diction structure, poor choice of words, and a limited vocabulary.

"My long-term career goal?....Actually, I want to get your job."

Appropriate Appearance

A job candidate who doesn't take the time to put the right foot forward by maintaining a proper appearance probably doesn't have the wherewithal to perform adequately in the job. Clean, appropriate clothing and proper grooming show that the candidate is willing to make the effort to please the employer. Candidates who are sloppy in appearance and mannerisms will bring those characteristics to the job and to their interactions with other parts of the company.

Make sure your UNIX programmer understands proper dress codes.

Savvy professionals will adopt the dress of the executive and banking industry. This attire generally includes:

- Crisp white shirt
- Conservative tie
- Dark suit
- Dark leather shoes

Proper job interview attire is important.

We will take a closer look at the on-site interview in the next chapter.

Conducting the Background Check

As we have repeatedly noted, a candidate's references must always be rigorously checked. Previous employers should be spoken with, if possible, to learn about a candidate's past work history. Many people are good at interviewing but won't necessarily function in the job.

Because of the explosive growth of the IT industry, fraudulent résumés have become increasingly common. Job candidates have been known to fabricate their college educations and the scope of their work experience, smooth over gaps in their employment history, and exaggerate their job skills. In some cases, job skills may be exaggerated inadvertently, because the job candidate has only a brief exposure to a technology and does not understand their own limitations.

Therefore, it is very important for the HR department to perform a complete resume check before forwarding any of these candidates for detailed interviews by the IT manager. These background checks may require the candidate's waiver signature for the release of all medical, criminal, and credit-related records.

The high rate of fraud found in resume applications has spawned a new industry of private investigators, who for a fixed fee, will check national databases, revealing any criminal activity on the part of the job candidate, a history of bad credit, and other moral and demographic factors that may be relevant to their suitability for the position.

Making the Initial Job Offer

Once the IT manager has chosen the first candidate, it is common to make an offer based on nation-wide studies of the average salaries within the geographical area. For example, IT professionals in expensive urban areas, such as New York City, will earn twice as much as an IT professional with the same skills, working in a cheaper suburban or rural area.

If you decide to make an offer to a candidate, it is a good idea to ask them the salary amount they have in mind. If the candidate is the first to mention a number, the company is placed in an advantageous negotiating position.

If the candidate indicates he will be satisfied with an amount that is lower than you were prepared to offer, then you have arrived at the ideal hiring scenario. You have a candidate that you have already decided is desirable for the position, and they will take less money than you had anticipated paying them.

On the other hand, if the candidate has an unreasonably high expectation given his Skill level and the market in your area, he may have an unrealistic view of the current business environment. This can indicate either that the candidate didn't do his homework or simple wishful thinking. You might point out that the range for this position is somewhat lower than he anticipates. You can then offer the amount you originally had in mind, and negotiate from there.

The savvy IT manager will try to offer a candidate with an excellent set of IT skills a balance between the "going rate" and other intangible benefits, in order to make the job appealing. Other intangibles might include additional vacation time, flextime, telecommuting, additional vacation days, and other perks designed to make the job more attractive to the candidates. Of course, the IT manager may deliberately reduce the size of the initial offer if he anticipates that the candidate may negotiate for more. A highly desirable IT candidate may be courted by multiple companies and will often respond to the job offer with a counteroffer, citing other employers who are willing to pay more for the same skill set. When this happens, the IT manager may soon be faced with the dilemma of paying more than they desired for the candidate, and may also question the candidate's motive in earning a high salary.

Conclusion

In sum, while the recession of 2002-3 has created a shakeout within the lower ranks of system administrators, IT managers remain committed to retaining their top system administration talent, and those professionals with specialized skills are still in high demand.

In today's highly volatile work environment, the average IT professional rarely stays with a single employer for a long period of time. Competition remains extremely strong for those system administration superstars whose skill and background make them indispensable. While some attrition of IT professionals is inevitable, there are many techniques that savvy IT managers can use to retain their top talent.

At this point, you should be ready to invite the candidate for an on-site interview. Let's look at an approach to conducting a technical interview to access the candidate's level of technical knowledge.

The On-site Interview

Tailoring the Interview

During the on-site interview, the candidate needs to be evaluated for both technical skills and non-technical personality traits that will indicate whether the candidate can be successful in the work environment.

Now it's your turn to ask the tough questions!

The specific areas that you choose to emphasize in the interview will depend on the nature of the position. A project manager who coordinates the efforts of several people will need a different skill set than someone who primarily works only with data. Choose questions that will highlight the specific skills you need and look for past experiences that demonstrate those abilities.

An effective IT manager must be able to wear many hats. He must have the creative vision necessary for planning projects, the interpersonal skills involved in communicating with a project team and coordinating their efforts, and he must serve as a liaison between upper management and the people who implement the project. Ask questions that demonstrate these abilities and look for experiences that show accomplishments in these areas.

Questions from the Candidate

Most books and articles neglect to discuss the questions that the candidate may ask the interviewer. This is unfortunate, because whether or not the candidate asks questions, and the character of those questions, can reveal a lot about his personality and suitability for the job.

After all, the serious candidate is evaluating the company just as you are evaluating him. If he is able to ask intelligent questions that are intended to assess how well his particular abilities and goals will integrate with the job, he is actually doing part of your job for you.

A certain amount of nervousness is inherent to the interview process, but the passive candidate who appears reluctant or unable to answer interview questions, as if under cross-examination, can only raise suspicions about the reason for his reticence. Contrast this person with the engaging candidate who doesn't answer so much as he conversationally responds, volunteering the pertinent information while interspersing his responses with questions of his own.

The candidate's questions should focus on the tasks and responsibilities he will encounter in the performance of his job. If the candidate takes the initiative in this way, facilitating the interview as you mutually explore whether the position is a good fit, chances are he will bring this same constructive approach to the work environment once you determine that he is, indeed, the best person for the job.

Beware of the candidate who only seems to be interested in his salary and the other perks that he will enjoy. There will be time to discuss money once you both decide that the alliance between you is promising. The thrust of the interview should be on the requirements of the position and whether the candidate is equipped to meet them.

Technical Questions

The following questions were developed in case no one in your organization is qualified to assess the job candidate's skill set. Even without detailed knowledge of UNIX, you can get a vague idea of the technical skills of your system administrator job candidate.

While this quick technical check can be administered over the telephone, it is often performed on-site by a certified system administrator. Each question is unambiguous with a clear answer.

The interviewer should begin by apologizing for asking pointed technical questions before reading each question verbatim. If a candidate asks for clarification or says that he or she does not understand the question, the interviewer re-reads the question. If the candidate fails to answer a question or answers incorrectly, the interviewer should respond "OK," and move immediately to the next question.

IMPORTANT NOTE:

The intention of this section is not to provide a comprehensive UNIX technical exam, and the technical questions in this section are only intended to be examples. The only way to accurately evaluate the technical skills of a job applicant is to employ the services of an experienced system administrator and conduct an in-depth technical interview and skills assessment.

Also note that the expected answers from the questions are highly dependent upon the flavor of UNIX. We have tried to make the questions as neutral as possible, but each vendor introduces their own features into the standard UNIX toolkit, and these example questions may not be appropriate for your version of UNIX. An experienced system administrator should administer the interview questions presented in this book.

Qualifications

1. Do you have any Certifications? (i.e. Java Programmer/Developer, Cisco, Microsoft, Oracle)

   Answer: _____

   _____

   Comment: _____

2. Highest level of education?

   The job typically requires a college education, preferably a BS in computer science or related engineering field.

   Answer: _____

   _____

   Comment: _____

UNIX telephone pre-screen questions

1. What is the default windowing system used in UNIX?

   Expected answer: X Windows

   Score: _____

   Comment: _____

   _____

2. What command is used to list the contents of a directory?

   Expected answer: ls

   Score: _____

   Comment: _____

   _____

3. What command is used to display a list of currently running processes?

   Expected answer: ps

   Score: _____

   Comment: _____

   _____

4. What is a login shell?

   Expected answer:
   The login shell is the program that is executed when a user logs into the system. This program accepts user commands and executes them. This is the main user interface to the operating system. Examples of shells include bash, sh, tcsh, csh and ksh.

Score: _____

Comment: _____

_____

5. What is a UID?

Expected answer:
UID stands for User Identification. It is the unique number that is assigned to every user on a UNIX system.

Score: _____

Comment: _____

_____

6. In what file is the relationship of UID to username defined?

Expected answer: /etc/passwd

Score: _____

Comment: _____

_____

7. What command is used to check a filesystem for errors?

Expected answer: fsck

Score: _____

Comment: _____

_____

8. Is there a difference between a file called OUTPUT.TXT (in all caps) and output.txt (all lowercase) in UNIX?

Expected answer:
Yes. UNIX operating systems are case sensitive.

      Score: _____

   Comment: _____

            _____

9. What command is used to read the manual page for a given command?

   Expected answer: man <command>

      Score: _____

   Comment: _____

            _____

10. What symbol is used to redirect standard out (STDOUT) to a file?

   Expected answer: > (the greater-than sign)

      Score: _____

   Comment: _____

            _____

11. What command is used to establish a secure command-line session with another system over a TCP/IP network?

   Expected answer: ssh

      Score: _____

   Comment: _____

            _____

12. What file contains the list of drives that are mounted at boot?

Expected answer:
Solaris: /etc/vfstab
Other UNIX: /etc/fstab

Score: _____

Comment: _____

_____

13. In what file is the default runlevel defined?

Expected answer: /etc/inittab

Score: _____

Comment: _____

_____

Security

1. Define and describe TCP Wrappers. What are the reasons for using TCP Wrappers in addition to a host-based firewall?

   Skill level: High

   Expected answer:

   > TCP Wrappers is a tool used to restrict inbound access to network services. Using the files /etc/hosts.deny and /etc/hosts.allow, a system administrator can define what range of IP addresses or hosts are allowed or denied access to certain ports on a system.
   >
   > TCP Wrappers does not replace a firewall! For one thing, TCP Wrappers will only protect those services that query it to control access. A common program that does this is inetd, the internet superserver.
   >
   > So why use TCP Wrappers in addition to a firewall? TCP Wrappers provide a second line of defense in the event the firewall is compromised. TCP Wrappers also offer excellent logging capabilities, giving you a way to verify your firewall logs.

   Score: _____

   Comment: _____

   _____

2. Define and discuss the security ramifications of each of these situations:

   Current directory (".") in root's $PATH variable
   "r" commands (rlogin, rcp, etc)
   setUID bit on /bin/vi

Skill level: High

Expected answer:

If an administrator is coming from the DOS or Windows world, he is probably surprised when he tries to execute a binary in his current working directory and he receives the error "command not found". Unlike DOS and Windows, the current working directory is not in a user's $PATH by default. This means that in order to run the program /home/bin/program, you must either type the full path name at the command line, cd to /home/bin and type "./program", or add /home/bin/ to your $PATH variable.

It is possible to replicate this windows functionality on UNIX systems. In UNIX, the current working directory can be referred to with the period ("."). To make the UNIX command line work like the Windows one, you could issue the command "PATH=.:$PATH". This will set the current directory to be the first place that the shell searches for binaries when you issue a command.

This, however, is an enormous security risk. In a multi-user environment like UNIX, you must always be aware that other people are using the same system. If a root user were to alter his $PATH this way, a malicious user could create a file in the /tmp directory called 'ls'. This file could be a shell script that could do anything at all, even deleting the entire system. If this is made executable, and the root user changed directories to /tmp and issued the 'ls' command, the malicious script is executed (as root) instead of the system /bin/ls.

The "r" commands have been popular for many years on UNIX systems. These commands exist to give remote access to users using multiple UNIX systems.

There are two inherent flaws with these commands that make them essentially useless in a secure networking environment. First, these command all transmit data over the network in plain text. Anyone running a packet sniffer that has access to the same network segment will see all of the data being transmitted. Second, the authentication system for these commands is based on restricting and allowing access by IP address only. It is far too easy to spoof an IP address, meaning that unauthorized access to these services is relatively simple.

In order to achieve the same functionality that these commands offer, but to do it in a secure way, install the OpenSSH software suite. This package is an open-source implementation of the ssh (secure shell) applications and other similar applications. Not only does ssh encrypt all data that is sent over the network, it supports more advanced authentication mechanisms, such as public/private key based authentication.

It is very important that the setUID bit be used with care. The UNIX permissions model is based on a parent-child relationship. When a parent process spawns a child process, the child process inherits the permissions of the parent. For example, if an application gives the user an option of spawning a shell, that applications can never be assigned the setUID bit. If it were, the shell that it spawned would have the permissions of root, giving any user full access to the system. In the same vein, an application like the vi editor can never be setUID, since it would then allow any user to modify any file on the system, completely bypassing the UNIX security model.

Score: _____

Comment: _____

_____

3. What is the advantage of giving a user elevated privileges to certain commands through sudo, as opposed to giving them root access to a system?

Skill level: Intermediate

Expected answer:

With the sudo command, it is easy to limit what command a user may run as root through entires in the /etc/sudoers file. This allows a system administrator to create varying levels of access for certain users, without having to give out the root password.

Sudo also logs every attempted access and every command that it runs, leaving a detailed audit trail behind for all programs run with superuser privileges.

Score: _____

Comment: _____

_____

4. What is the chroot command and why is it important to the security of a system?

Skill level: Intermediate

Expected answer:

The chroot command stands for 'change root'. This command allows a system administrator to set up a restricted section of the filesystem for users to use (commonly called a 'chroot jail'). This filesystem appears to the user to be the complete filesystem, but in reality it is merely a subdirectory of the 'real' filesystem, containing just those commands and directories that the system administrator wishes the user to have access to.

Although the UNIX permissions model is a tried and true one, it is still fraught with enough complications that few system administrators would feel comfortable with strange users roaming through their machines. Chroot gives them the ability to grant access to certain users, but to limit that access in such a restrictive way that the user cannot access something the administrator does not want them to access.

Chroot is also commonly used when running system services. Most UNIX system services run as the root user. This makes these services extremely vulnerable to buffer overflow attacks. If a buffer overflow attack succeeds, the attacker will be left with a shell on the system that has inherited the permissions of the service owner (in this case, root). However, if the service is run in its own chroot jail, the damage caused by these kinds of attacks is greatly minimized, because the attacker is left with an extremely limited shell as opposed to their entire filesystem.

Score: _____

Comment: _____

_____

5. Describe a buffer overflow attack and list possible defenses.

Skill level: High

Expected answer:

A buffer overflow attack is perhaps the most common system compromise in the history of computing security. When a programmer writes software that expects input, that expected input is assigned a buffer in the system. The size of that buffer is dependent upon the expected size of the data. If the programmer has not put checks in place to validate the size of the input data, a malicious user can send more data than can be allocated in the buffer, causing an overflow. In the best case, this will cause memory corruption in the program and it will fail. In the worst case, specific data can be sent in the overflow portion of the input data, which is then executed with the privileges of the owner of the program. In the case of a system service running as root, a remote buffer overflow attack can allow an attacker to run arbitrary code as the root user on a system.

The real defense against a buffer overflow attack is to prevent them from ever happening. This can be accomplished through a complete code audit, ensuring that every data input point in an application does proper bounds checking to ensure that only the amount of data that can be allocated is accepted. In practice, this is often difficult to do, even with the available code profiling tools available.

A common practice is to treat this kind of attack like any other in the networking security realm – assume it will happen and make plans to identify it and reduce the damage. Identification is normally handled by examining the logs of a system, looking for strange log entires from a system service. If a system has been compromised, file system integrity tools will tell you what files on the system have been modified. A chroot jail is commonly used to minimize the amount of damage that is possible from an attack of this nature. This has become a common enough solution that some popular server programs have built-in chroot functionality (sendmail is an example).

In Linux, there are kernel modules available to assist in the defense against buffer overflow attacks. These patches go about this in different ways, but most focus on preventing arbitrary code from being inserted onto the stack and executed, making traditional buffer overflow attacks much more difficult to execute.

Score: _____

Comment: _____

_____

6. What is the weakest point in any network or system's security? What can you do about it?

Skill level: Low

Expected answer:

People. No matter how much money you have spent on the latest in firewalls, intrusion detection tools, forensic analysis and physical security, people are always the weakest link. This is a fundamental rule of computer security that everyone who works in the field needs to realize. Simply having an easy-to-guess password can completely compromise the security infrastructure of an entire organization.

What is the answer to this problem? Education. An educated user is much less of a security risk. Security is a tricky thing when it comes to users: be too lenient, and they will ignore it. Be too stringent, and they will do everything in their power to bypass is. Finding the right balance is a challenge. The first step to this is educating your work force. Telling a user why the company's password policy should be followed, instead of threatening to fire them if they disobey, you will probably get a better response. Security needs to be a standard part of everyone's job. In this day and age, everyone is responsible for the security of a company's systems and data. By letting a user know what is acceptable and what isn't, you will go a long way towards making your environment a much more secure place.

Score: _____

Comment: _____

_____

7. Describe a file system integrity tool and explain its importance.

Skill level: Intermediate

Expected answer:

A file system integrity tool is an application that maintains a record of all the files on a system. This record will contain every bit of data about each file, including time stamp, size, owner, location, etc. Periodically, a check of the existing file system against this record is run. If part of the filesystem has been modified, it will not match this record, and the system administrator will be notified.

This is an important tool because YOUR SYSTEMS WILL GET BROKEN INTO! It is not a question of IF; it is only a question of WHEN. Assuming that you alone have an infallible security model is the equivalent of refusing to face reality. Due to some error, either human, hardware, or software, your systems will be compromised. The largest problem that arises from this event is the time it takes the system administrator to figure out that a compromise took place. Stories abound of companies finding out months later that they were compromised, after the attacker stole all of their data and used their systems to attack other systems on the internet.

A file system integrity tool will notify you if a part of your system has been modified. It is the first step in recovering from an intrusion.

Score: _____

Comment: _____

_____

8. What is an intrusion detection system and what are some basic flaws in the concept of 'detecting intrusion'?

Skill level: High

Expected answer:

An intrusion detection system (IDS) is software that monitors a system or network, looking for evidence of activity that can be identified as malicious.

There are a number of different kinds of IDS systems available. The simplest of these will monitor system log files looking for any suspicious messages generated by the system services. A second type of IDS will monitor the activity of a network or system and match what it finds against a pattern of known 'attack signatures'. Similar to anti-virus programs, these IDS systems are able to identify an intrusion if it follows the pattern of a previously known attack. The third kind of IDS system is also similar to an anti-virus program. Many anti-virus programs use heuristic analysis to identify programs that 'look like' viruses. In this same way, an IDS can identify system activity that appears to be malicious but does not match any known malicious pattern.

The inherent flaw in all of these systems is that it is very difficult to write an algorithm that can differentiate between 'good' and 'bad' activity. Since these systems do not take into account the context of a pattern, there can be many false positives. An IDS system that generates too many false positives is worse than no IDS system at all. A system administrator will simply start to delete all of the notifications while believing that his network and systems are secure.

Although flawed, when configured correctly and kept up to date, IDS systems can be an important piece in the overall security plan of an organization.

Score: _____

Comment: _____

_____

9. What is ARP cache poisoning, and how can it be prevented?

Skill level: High

Expected answer:

The ARP (Address Resolution Protocol) cache on a system is what translates IP addresses to MAC addresses on a local TCP/IP network. It is relatively easy to spoof ARP replies, meaning that if one system on your network is compromised, that system can spoof other systems on the network easily. Your server will think that it is connecting to a trusted host, when in reality it is connecting to the compromised system, or even worse, another host on the Internet.

To prevent this from happening, you can define a list of systems that your server must trust. In the file /etc/ethers, you can hard code the MAC address to IP address mapping of these systems, preventing ARP from overriding this information. This disadvantage of this approach is that if the network card changes in any of these systems, the MAC address will change as well, meaning this file must be updated.

Score: _____

Comment: _____

_____

10. Describe VPN technology and list some common implementations.

Skill level: Intermediate

Expected answer:

A VPN (Virtual Private Network) is an encrypted tunnel that exists to transmit data over an otherwise insecure public network. VPNs are most commonly used to transmit secure data over the internet. Instead of handling the encryption and authentication at the application layer (like SSL enabled web sites), a VPN handles all encryption at the network layer, allowing traditional networking protocols to use the VPN tunnel without modification.

There are three common VPN solutions in use today:

- IPSec based solutions. IPSec is the security protocol built into the next version of IP, Ipv6. Many vendors have standardized on IPSec as their VPN solution, including Cisco and Sun Microsystems.

- PPTP based solutions. The Point to Point Tunneling Protocol is a modification to the standard PPP protocol which allows for encryption and authentication at the network layer. PPTP support is built into later version of Microsoft Windows, and implementations are available for most UNIX operating systems.

- Proprietary solutions. Since a VPN tunnel is essentially just encrypted traffic, any reliable encryption algorithm can be used to create a tunnel. It is even possible to use the encryption functionality of the ssh application to build a VPN tunnel.

Score: _____

Comment: _____

_____

11. What is a DMZ and why would you want one?

Skill level: Intermediate

Expected answer:

DMZ stands for Demilitarized Zone. This is a term that describes a small network that exists between a corporate network and the internet. The DMZ will house publically available servers, such as web servers and mail servers. Users inside the company network can access hosts in the DMZ, and users outside the company network can access hosts inside the DMZ, but the DMZ acts as a buffer between the company network and the internet. If a host in the DMZ is compromised, the attacker will not gain access to any server inside the company.

Score: _____

Comment: _____

_____

12. On Linux, how can the directory entires at the top of the /proc filesystem aid in security?

Skill level: High

Expected answer:

When a system is compromised, a rootkit is commonly installed by the intruder. A rootkit is a set of trojaned programs that replace common system programs. An example would be a trojaned version of the 'login' program which always accepts a certain username/password combination. Another example is a trojaned version of the 'ps' program which will display all running processes except the ones that the attacker wished to hide.

The first step in security is knowledge. What is running on your system? Traditionally, the 'ps' command is used to display this information. But what if you don't trust the 'ps' command? In this case, you need a deeper understanding of how the operating system works. In Linux, all of the informational commands are simply frontends for data that is available as text files or directories in the /proc filesystem. Specifically, every running process on a Linux system will have a directory under /proc. For example, the init process (PID #1), will have a directory of /proc/1. So if you are ever in doubt about the reliability of the 'ps' command, compare its output with the directories in

/proc. If you see a discrepancy, you probably have a compromised system.

Score: _____

Comment: _____

_____

The moral of this story is that there is no such thing as too much knowledge. By having a good understanding of how things work behind the scenes, you are better able to handle unexpected situations.

Networking Questions

1. What command is used to display the ports that are open on a UNIX system?

    Skill level: Low

    Expected answer:

    The 'netstat' command will display all open ports and all network connections.

    Score: _____

    Comment: _____

    _____

2. What is the subnet mask for a default Class-C IP network?

    Skill level: Low

    Expected answer:

    255.255.255.0

    Score: _____

    Comment: _____

    _____

3. In a standard class C IP network, how many IP addresses can be assigned to hosts? What are the other nonassignable addresses used for?

    Skill level: Intermediate

    Expected answer:

    A Class C network has a total of 256 (2^8) IP addresses. However, only 254 of these can be assigned to hosts. The first IP address in the subnet is the network IP address, which is used to refer to the network as a whole. The last IP address in the subnet is the broadcast address, which is used to communicate with each host on the network.

Score: _____

Comment: _____

_____

4. What is a MAC address?

Skill level: Low

Expected answer:

A MAC (Media Access Control) address is a 48-bit address that is assigned to every hardware device that is designed to communicate on an ethernet network. Hardware manufacturers are assigned a range of MAC addresses to use for their products to ensure uniqueness.

Score: _____

Comment: _____

_____

5. You wish to set up a Linux system as a router between two subnets. You have installed and configured two network cards, each attached to a different subnet. What are the steps that need to occur before the system will act as a router?

Skill level : Intermediate

Expected answer:

Step 1: You must configure the packet forwarding rules. In recent versions of the Linux kernel (2.4 and later) this is accomplished with the 'iptables' command.

Step 2: You must instruct the kernel to forward packets between the two interfaces. This is accomplished with this command:

echo 1 > /proc/sys/net/ipv4/ip_forward

Score: _____

Comment: _____

_____

6. What is an MTU?

Skill level: Intermediate

Expected answer:

The MTU (Maximum Transmission Unit) is the largest packet size that can be sent over a TCP/IP network. If a packet is larger than the MTU of the operating system or router, it will get broken into smaller packets. You can often increase network performance by ensuring that your operating system is using the same size MTU as your local router.

Score: _____

Comment: _____

_____

7. What file determines the DNS servers that are queried when a network request is made?

Skill level : Low

Expected answer:

/etc/resolv.conf

Score: _____

Comment: _____

_____

8. What is the difference between UDP and TCP?

Skill level: Intermediate

Expected answer:

UDP and TCP are both Layer 4 (Transport) protocols in the IP protocol stack. UDP (User Datagram Protocol) is considered an 'unreliable' protocol because it does no end-to-end verification or packet numbering during transmission. The higher-level application that utilizes UDP must be responsible for the reassembly of the UDP packets. Examples of UDP based services are tftp and nfs.

TCP (Transmission Control Protocol) is considered a reliable protocol because it has built in tools for guaranteeing delivery of packets and a system for requesting the resending of a packet if packet loss occurs. Because of this, TCP incurs more overhead then UDP. Examples of TCP based services are smtp and http.

Score: _____

Comment: _____

_____

9. What steps are necessary to configure a Solaris system to participate in an IP network?

Skill level: Intermediate

Expected answer:

This assumes that the Solaris system is not part of an NIS/NIS+ network.

- /etc/hosts must contain the hostname and IP address of the system.

- /etc/hostname.\<interface\> must contain the hostname of the system. \<interface\> is the corresponding interface; for example,

- /etc/hostname.dmfe0

- /etc/netmasks must contain the subnet mask for the system.

- If using DNS, /etc/resolv.conf needs to contain the primary DNS server.

- /etc/defaultrouter must contain the IP address of the router for the subnet.

Score: _____

Comment: _____

_____

10. What is TCP sequence number prediction and what can you do to prevent it?

Skill level: High

Expected answer:

Since TCP is a reliable protocol, each TCP packet is assigned a sequence number. It's the responsibility of the receiving end of a TCP connection to put the incoming packets in order, and re-request a packet if one got lost along the way. Theoretically, if a third system can successfully trick one of the two systems in a TCP conversation into communicating with it instead of the original system, the third system can break into the conversation. This is known as 'session hijacking', or the 'man-in-the-middle' attack. In order for this attack to work, the third system has to know the TCP sequencing being used between the original systems. If this sequencing is based on a known algorithm, determining the next TCP sequence number is trivial and this attack becomes easier.

This vulnerability didn't come to light until around the year 2000. At that time, most UNIX vendors issued patches to their kernels to ensure that the algorithm used to calculate TCP sequence numbers was more complicated. There are, however, many systems on the internet today that are still vulnerable to this kind of attack. The moral of the story is: keep your systems updated.

Score: _____

Comment: _____

_____

11. You have purchased a domain name and setup one of your UNIX servers as a DNS server. What entry must you make in your primary zone file to ensure that email addressed to your domain is sent to the correct mail server?

Skill level: Intermediate

Expected answer:

The MX record is the DNS entry that is responsible for defining the mail server for a particular domain. It is recommended that a domain have multiple MX records for the sake of redundancy.

12. Associate these common network services with their default
    port numbers

    Telnet
    SSH
    FTP
    SMTP
    DNS
    POP3
    HTTP
    HTTPS
    IMAP

Skill level: Intermediate

Expected answer:

Obviously, one is not expected to memorize all of the
common port numbers and services. However, these are
common enough that all good UNIX system
administrators should know them by heart.

Telnet:	TCP 23
SSH:	TCP 22
FTP:	TCP 20 & TCP 21
SMTP:	TCP 25
DNS:	TCP 53 and UDP 53
POP3:	TCP 110
HTTP:	TCP 80
HTTPS:	TCP 443
IMAP:	TCP 143

Score: _____

Comment: _____

_____

13. What command will display the routing table on a UNIX system?

Skill level: Low

Expected answer:

netstat -r

Score: _____

Comment: _____

_____

14. Your UNIX system is able to ping other devices on the local subnet, but it is unable to ping a device outside of the subnet. What could be the problem?

Skill level: Intermediate

Expected answer:

In order for a host to communicate outside of its subnet, it must know the default router to the address. This error could indicate that the default router is not set or is incorrect. If the default router setting on the host is correct, then there may be a problem with the router itself.

Score: _____

Comment: _____

_____

15. When you initiate a telnet session to your UNIX system, the connection is established, but there is a 20 second or more pause before you see a login prompt. What could cause this?

Skill level: High

Expected answer:

The telnet server performs a reverse DNS query on every IP address that attempts a connection. If DNS is configured incorrectly, or the DNS for the network is down, the server will wait for a DNS timeout before presenting a login prompt to the telnet client.

Score: _____

Comment: _____

_____

System Adminstration

1. Describe the default partitioning scheme in Solaris, denoting the slice number, the default mount point, and the purpose.

   Skill level: High

   Expected answer:

   - Slice 0 is mounted as the root partition (/) by default. This is the top level UNIX file system.

   - Slice 1 is reserved for swap space. The size of this will depend upon the amount of memory and the duties the system will perform.

   - Slice 2 represents the entire disk and is not mounted.

   - Slice 3 is mounted as /export by default. Commonly used to hold exported information, such as user home directories or alternative versions of operating system binaries.

   - Slice 4 is mounted as /export/swap by default. This partition is used to provide virtual memory space for client systems. Slice 4 is also commonly mounted as /opt.

   - Slice 5 is mounted as /opt by default. This is where packages are installed that are not critical to the functioning of Solaris. If /opt was mounted already as Slice 4, this slice is often mounted as /var.

   - Slice 6 is mounted as /usr by default. /usr contains binaries and libraries that are used by normal system users. /usr is commonly shared between systems.

   - Slice 7 is mounted as /home, /export/home or /export/spare by default. Commonly holds user directories or other shared information.

2. Define and describe the following terms related to disk management under UNIX:

Boot block
Super block
Logical block
Inode

Skill level: Intermediate

Expected answer:

The boot block (or master boot record on intel-based systems) stores the information needed to boot the system. The data starts at sector (or cylinder group) 0 and can reside on any disk that the hardware is capable of booting from. For example, if you're using Linux on an x86 based system, and your system BIOS supports booting off of a usb drive, you can use a removable usb drive as your boot device.

The super block contains information about the file system itself. This information includes:

■ file system size and status

■ file system label

■ file system state (clean, dirty)

■ logical block size

Without the superblock, the file system is unusable. Because of its importance, when a file system is created on a disk, multiple copies of the superblock are created on different parts of the disk for use in case the main superblock becomes corrupted.

A logical block is the smallest unit of data that can be stored on a file system. The size of the logical block on a particular file system is determined when that file system is created. Common sizes for logical blocks are 8K, 4K, 2K, 1K and 512 bytes. If you save a file that is smaller than the logical block size, the file will still take up one logical block of space.

An inode (or index node) contains all of the information about a file except the filename itself. Every file on a UNIX system has an inode, containing information such as:

- Type of file (regular, directory, link, character special, etc)

- Last access time, last modified time, creation time

- Size of the file

- Permissions and ownership of the file

The number of inodes allocated to a file system is fixed at the time the file system is created. If this number is exceeded, no new files can be created on the file system, even if there is free space available.

Score: _____

Comment: _____

_____

3. Describe the processes for adding a new hard disk to a Unix system.

Skill level: Intermediate

Expected answer:

Step 1: Physically install the hard disk in the machine. If it is an IDE disk, ensure that the proper master/slave jumper settings are set. If it is a SCSI disk, ensure that a unique LUN is used and that termination on the SCSI chain is correct.

Step 2: Partition the disk. Use the 'format' command on Solaris or the 'fdisk' command on Linux or BSD systems.

Step 3: Create a file system on the disk. On Solaris and BSD, use the 'newfs' command. On Linux, use the 'mkfs' command appropriate for the file system type (ie mke2fs, mkreiserfs, etc).

Step 4: If it doesn't already exist, create a mountpoint for the new disk. mkdir /mnt/newdisk

Step 5: Ensure that the disk mounts automatically when the system boots. On Solaris, add an entry to /etc/vfstab. On BSD and Linux, add an entry to /etc/fstab.

Step 6: Mount the file system. mount /mnt/newdisk

Score: _____

Comment: _____

_____

4. What is the difference between a regular file system and a journalling file system?

Skill level: Intermediate

Expected answer:

In today's world, all file systems take advantage of a write cache, meaning that requests to write to the disk are actually written to memory first. The kernel then decides when to flush this cache to the disk (normally when there is some level of system downtime). This speeds up the overall performance of the system. The problem with this method arises when a disk is unmounted or becomes unavailable before the cache is flushed. This can happen if power is lost or a system failure occurs. When this happens, before the disk can be mounted again, it must be scanned in order to analyze the disk and bring it back to a consistent state. With large disks, this can take a significant amount of time, during which the system is unavailable.

In order to address this problem, journaling file systems were developed. By borrowing a technology present in the database world for many years (transaction logs), a file system is able to recover much more quickly from an unplanned failure. Instead of scanning the entire disk, only the transaction log is examined, reducing the recovery time from possibly hours to seconds.

Score: _____

Comment: _____

_____

5. Define and describe the common UNIX file systems.

Skill level: High

Expected answer:

- UFS – The UNIX file system. The original standard for UNIX file systems and the default on BSD and Solaris, it is based on the original BSD FAT Fast file system.

- JFS – Journaling file system. This file system was developed by IBM and is the default file system under AIX. IBM has also ported this file system to Linux.

- EXT2 – The standard Linux file system. This is a non-journaling file system.

- EXT3 – EXT2 with journaling capabilities.

- XFS – Silicon Graphics' journaling file system. XFS is the default file system in IRIX and has also been ported to Linux.

- ReiserFS – Journaling file system developed by Hans Reiser. Touted for its speed and scalability. Available in most Linux distributions.

Score: _____

Comment: _____

_____

6. What are the 3 settings in the standard UNIX file permissions model, and how does each apply to files and directories?

Skill level: Intermediate

Expected answer:

For files:

- Read – Can open the file and read its contents
- Write – Can modify the file
- Execute – Can execute the file

For directories:

- Read – Can list the files in a directory
- Write – Can add or removes file from the directory
- Execute – Can execute a program within the current contents of the directory

Directory permissions are a little non-intuitive. For example, it's not immediately obvious what the 'execute' option on a directory would give you, since you can't actually execute a directory. It does not mean that you can execute binaries that are inside that directory. If you do not have execute permissions on a directory, you will not, for example, be able to list the contents of that directory. Because the 'ls' command needs to run against the directory in question, the command 'ls <directory>' will be denied.

A frequently asked question about UNIX permissions is "How do I grant the 'change' option to a user?" UNIX doesn't have a 'change' bit, but you can replicate the functionality within the existing permissions model. 'Change' means that you can't delete a file, but you can modify it. To replicate this in UNIX, you first ensure that the user has write access to the file itself. This allows them to modify the file. Then, to ensure that they can't remove it, revoke their write privileges on the directory that houses the file. This will prevent them from removing the file itself.

Score: _____

Comment: _____

_____

7. What is the setUID bit and how is it employed?

Skill level: Intermediate

Expexted answer:

When the setUID bit is enabled for an executable file, that file will execute with the permissions of the file owner rather than the permissions of the parent process. This is useful for enabling regular users to run privileged commands without having to give them root access.

setUID is set with the chmod command. To change the permissions on an executable file so the setUID bit is set, owner has read, write and execute, group has read, write and other has read and write, issue the following command:

chmod 4755 <filename>

Score: _____

Comment: _____

_____

8. Define and describe the cron job scheduling system. What are the fields available to define the time a job will execute?

Skill level: High

Expected answer:

Cron is the default UNIX job scheduler. Cron jobs are defined per user in /var/spool/cron/<username>. This file lists each user's cron jobs, one per line. Each line contains 6 fields:

- Field 1 – Minute
- Field 2 – Hour
- Field 3 – Day of the month
- Field 4 – Month
- Field 5 – Day of the week
- Field 6 – Program to run

By default, any output sent to STDOUT or STDERR from these scheduled programs is emailed to the user.

Score: _____

Comment: _____

_____

9. How do you disable a user account without deleting it? Assume shadow passwords are being used.

Skill level: Low

Expected answer:

The command 'passwd -l <username>' will disable an account. It does this by placing an "!" in front of the user's encrypted password in the /etc/shadow file.

Score: _____

Comment: _____

_____

10. In the standard lpr-based UNIX printing system, what command will display the status of a print queue?

Skill level: Low

Expected answer:

lpq

Score: _____

Comment: _____

_____

11. Describe the Samba suite of utilities. How are they useful in a heterogeneous environment?

Skill level: Intermediate

Expected answer:

Samba is a software suite that implements the Server Message Block protocol on UNIX systems. This is the protocol that Microsoft Windows systems use for sharing filesharing, printer sharing, and authentication. The Samba server software allows a UNIX machine to act as a file, print, and authentication server for Windows clients. The Samba client software allows a UNIX machine to participate in a Windows network, accessing shared drives, printing to shared printers, and authenticating against a domain controller or an Active Directory server.

Score: _____

Comment: _____

_____

12. Describe the package management options available on Linux systems.

Skill level: Intermediate

Expected answer:

Most Linux distributions utilize either the rpm or the deb package format. Rpm based distributions include RedHat, SuSE and Mandrake. The Debian-based distributions utilize the deb package format, including Debian itself, Knoppix, Lindows and Xandros Linux. Both systems offer dependency checking, allowing for a level of intelligence when installing or upgrading software.

Score: _____

Comment: _____

_____

13. Describe the package management software on Solaris.

Skill level: Intermediate

Expected answer:

The pkgadd command is used to install software. When you receive a package from Sun, or download one from the internet, you install it with the 'pkgadd -d <package name>' command.

To see a list of packages installed on your Solaris system, run the command 'pkginfo'.

To list the files that belong to an installed package, run the command 'pkgchk -l <package name>'.

Score: _____

Comment: _____

_____

14. What are three ways to find a file on a UNIX system?

Skill level: Low

Expected answer:

The 'which' command will display the full path to a command if that command is in a directory defined by your $PATH environment variable.

The 'locate' command will query a hash database containing a list of all files on the filesystem. The database must be updated periodically. This command is not a standard part of all UNIX systems.

The 'find' command can search entire partitions for a file, using an exact or regular expression match.

15. If /etc/inittab defines your default runlevel as 3, where do your system startup scripts reside?

Skill level: Low

Expected answer:

/etc/rc3.d

Score: _____

Comment: _____

_____

16. You are logged in as root and wish to kill a process with PID #1054. You type 'kill 1054' but you still see the process in the process table. Why did the process not die, and what can you do to get rid of it?

Skill level: Intermediate

Expected answer:

When called with no arguments, the kill command by itself sends the TERM signal to a process. The TERM signal can be best described as 'asking the process to end when it's ready'. A process can be configured to specifically catch the TERM signal and ignore it. The process could also be in such a state that it is unable to respond to the TERM request. In this case, more drastic measures are called for. By passing the -9 option to kill ('kill -9 1054'), you are sending the KILL signal. This is a lower level signal that tells the kernel to terminate this process immediately. This is usually reserved for processes that are locked in some loop or wait state and do not heed the TERM signal. If a process does not respond to kill -9, it is usually in some non-recoverable state (like waiting on a disk that is no longer available). The only way to eliminate these processes is to reboot the system.

Score: _____

Comment: _____

_____

UNIX Commands and Files

The heart of the UNIX operating system is the command line. Having a good grasp of what commands are available is fundamental for working with a UNIX OS. In the same vein, since everything in UNIX is a file, knowledge of the file system is crucial. These questions can quickly weed out an experienced UNIX sysadmin from a trainee.

1. What are the fields defined in the /etc/passwd file?

   Skill level: Intermediate

   Expected answer:

   - Field 1: username
   - Field 2: placeholder for encrypted password (assuming shadow passwords are being used)
   - Field 3: UID (User Identification)
   - Field 4: GID (Group Identification)
   - Field 5: Comment
   - Field 6: Home directory
   - Field 7: Login shell

   Score: _____

   Comment: _____

   _____

2. What is the purpose of the 'grep' command?

   Skill level: Low

   Expected answer:

   grep is used to search for strings of text in files. Grep stands for 'Global Regular Expression Print'

Score: _____

Comment: _____

_____

3. What command is used to display information about the network interfaces on a system?

Skill level: Low

Expected answer:

ifconfig

Score: _____

Comment: _____

_____

4. The 'ps' command lists processes currently running on the system. Identify and describe the following column headers from the output of 'ps -aef':

- UID
- PID
- PPID
- TTY

Skill level: Intermediate

Expected answer:

- UID = User Identification, the owner of the process
- PID = Process ID. Each UNIX process is assigned a unique process ID.
- PPID = Parent Process ID. The PID of the parent of this process.

- TTY = On what terminal is this process running. If the TTY is "?", then the process is not running on a terminal (either a system process or a detached process).

Score: _____

Comment: _____

_____

5. In Solaris, what command is used to display the slice information for a particular disk?

Skill level: Low

Expected answer:

prtvtoc <device>

Score: _____

Comment: _____

_____

6. What command is used to display the disk space occupied by mounted file systems?

Skill level: Low

Expected answer:

df

Score: _____

Comment: _____

_____

7. What file contains a list of currently mounted file systems?

Skill level: Intermediate

Expected answer:

/etc/mtab (on Linux)
/etc/mnttab (on Solaris)

Score: _____

Comment: _____

_____

8. On Solaris, what file contains settings that define the default maximum time a password is valid and the default minimum time period before a password must be changed?

Skill level: Intermediate

Expected answer:

/etc/default/passwd

Score: _____

Comment: _____

_____

9. What command and options would you issue to set the permissions on a file to read, write, excute for owner, read and excute for group, and no permissions for other?

Skill level: Intermediate

Expected answer:

chmod 750 <filename>

10. What command will display the default file permissions that will be assigned when a user creates a file?

Skill level: Intermediate

Expected answer:

umask

11. On Solaris, what command is used to display the Access Control List entries for a file?

Skill level: Intermediate

Expected answer:

getfacl <filename>

12. What command is used to run an application with a different security context than the user's default? What is the configuration file for this command, where programs are listed which defined users can execute with higher privileges?

Skill level: Intermediate

Expected answer:

> sudo <program>
> /etc/sudoers

> Score: _____
>
> Comment: _____
>
> _____

13. What file defines the default runlevel of the system and dictates what directory holds the startup scripts for that runlevel?

Skill level: Low

Expected answer:

> /etc/inittab

> Score: _____
>
> Comment: _____
>
> _____

14. What command is used to check a filesystem for errors?

Skill level: Low

Expected answer:

> fsck

> Score: _____
>
> Comment: _____
>
> _____

15. Why are there normally two bin directories, /bin and /usr/bin?

Skill level: Intermediate

Expected answer:

The UNIX filesystem was designed to be shared by multiple systems. In a shared environment, it is unneccesary to have data duplication across multiple systems. The /usr partition on a UNIX system is designed to be shared by clients. This is normally accomplished by client systems mounting a server's /usr partition as their own. This way, all clients have access to the same programs without a system administrator having to maintain copies on multiple systems.

Because of this fact, files in the /usr partition must never be considered critical system files. If a client needs to boot up off of the network for some reason, they will not have access to their /usr partition if it is mounted from a central server. If some sort of system repair ability is necessary on a client system, that program needs to live in the /bin directory. By convention, the /bin directory is local to every system.

So the reason there are two bin directories is that /bin contains local system-level binaries that are ciritical for the correct operation of the system, while /usr/bin contains binaries that are less important and not ciritical to the basic functioning of the system.

Score: _____

Comment: _____

_____

16. On Solaris, what file defines the master kernel configuration file?

Skill level: Low

Expected answer:

/etc/system

Score: _____

Comment: _____

_____

17. At the Solaris OpenBoot prompt, what command will display all of the SCSI devices connected to the system?

Skill level: Intermediate

Expected answer:

probe-scsi

Score: _____

Comment: _____

_____

18. How do you boot a Solaris system into single user mode?

Skill level: Low

Expected answer:

- Get to the OpenBoot prompt by hitting Stop-A
- Boot the system with the command 'boot -s'

Score: _____

Comment: _____

_____

19. What command allows you display and to modify your keyboard mappings in X Windows?

Skill level: Intermediate

Expected answer:

xmodmap

Score: _____

Comment: _____

_____

20. In Linux, what file contains a list of all IRQs currently in use?

Skill level: High

Expected answer:

/proc/interrupts

Score: _____

Comment: _____

_____

Troubleshooting

1. You attempt to unmount a currently mounted disk and you receive the error "Unable to umount: device or resource busy". What does this mean and what must you do before you can unmount the disk?

Skill level: Intermediate

Expected answer:

> This means that some process is currently accessing the file system you are trying to unmount, either through an open file handle or having a process with a current working directory in the file system. You first need to identify what processes are accessing the file system and who owns those processes. You then must decide how to deal with those processes.

> The 'fuser' command will display the processes that are accessing a given file system. After you have determined what the processes are and who owns them, you can either 1) wait until those processes complete before you attempt to unmount the disk, 2) contact the user(s) in question to determine the status of the processes, or 3) kill the processes and unmount the disk.

Score: _____

Comment: _____

_____

2. You need to run the fsck program against a file system, but you must do this while the the file system is unmounted. Since the file system in question is the root file system, you cannot unmount it while the system is running. What options do you have for running fsck against this file system?

Skill level: Intermediate

Expected answer:

> There are two ways to get fsck to run against this file system when it is not mounted.
>
> - Access the disk from a different root partition. This can be done be either removing the disk itself and mounting it under another UNIX system, or booting your system with a root or rescue disk. Either way, you have access to the fsck command without relying on your original disk being mounted. You can then fsck the drive and return the system to its previous state.
>
> - Issue the command 'shutdown -r -F now'. The '-F' option to shutdown forces the system to run fsck against the drives defined in /etc/fstab (or /etc/vsftab) before they are mounted on the next reboot. The '-r' options tells shutdown to reboot the computer immediately.
>
> Score: _____
>
> Comment: _____
>
> _____

3. You have forgotten root's password. What options do you have to get back into the system as root?

Skill level: High

Expected answer:

> This answer will be higher-level to cover most flavors of UNIX; individual implementations will vary depending upon the UNIX flavor.
>
> Root's password is normally stored in encrypted form in either /etc/passwd or /etc/shadow. While it is impossible

to recover what the password was, you can change the password, or reset it to a null value.

The first step is to access the disk containing the root partition without booting to it. You can do this by either booting to a root rescue disk and then mounting the original root partition, or removing the drive itself and mounting it in another system. By accessing the root file system this way, you are bypassing any of the security on the file system itself.

When you have access to the root partition, locate the encrypted password string for root in /etc/passwd or /etc/shadow. Erase the encrypted string. Save your changes and return the system to its normal configuration (if you moved the disk, return it to the original system. If you booted off of a different boot disk, remove it and boot off of your original disk).

After rebooting, you should now be able to log in as root without giving a password. You can then reset root's password with the 'passwd' command.

Score: _____

Comment: _____

_____

4. Your UNIX workstation is unable to ping any hosts on the local TCP/IP network. What steps do you take to troubleshoot this problem?

Skill level: Intermediate

Expected answer:

This kind of question is a very revealing one. How a candidate answers this questions will determine their thought process, specifically how they approach a problem from a logical standpoint. Ideally, you want a candidate to display knowledge of what settings are necessary to enable communication on an IP network, but more importantly, you want them to follow the scientific method in diagnosing and resolving the problem.

The following items need to be correct in order to communicate on a local TCP/IP network:

- Some physical connection to the network, whether it be wired or wireless

- An IP address that is part of the local subnet, but is unique to that subnet

- A subnet mask that correctly reflects the configuration of the subnet

- A correct gateway IP address

- If name resolution is desired, a correct name server must be configured

From a troubleshooting standpoint, it's always best to start at the lowest level and work your way up. Before you can diagnose this problem, however, more information is required. Specifically, the candidate should ask these questions:

- What is the IP configuration of this subnet?

- What IP address, subnet mask, gateway and DNS address should be assigned to this workstation?

- What is the physical topology of the network?

- Is any other station on the network experiencing this problem?

This final question is key because you can spend all day troubleshooting a workstation, when in reality the problem lies elsewhere on the network.

Assuming the problem has been confined to the workstation itself, the basic troubleshooting can begin. Here are some example questions that should be asked by the candidate as they go through the troubleshooting process.

Is the physical cable connected to the network card? Is there a link light on the network card? Is there a corresponding link light on the port to which the cable is connected (on a switch or a hub)? Does the operating system recognize the network card (On Linux, the 'lspci' command will list all devices connected to the PCI bus. On Solaris, use the command 'prtconf -v').

Are the IP configuration settings correct? What does the command 'ifconfig -a' tell you? Is any Layer 2 traffic being seen (the command 'arp -a' will display the Layer 2 address resolution protocol table)?

Is any host-based firewall in effect that could be blocking pings? Is the system that you are trying to ping available and not blocking pings? Can you ping other hosts on the network?

As you can see, there are many possible solutions to this problem. A good candidate will understand the methodical steps involved in solving a problem of this nature, and will implement those steps in the most logical order.

5. Your production UNIX system has been running fine when users suddenly complain that the system is slow. You log in and the system feels 'sluggish' and the terminal is unable to keep up with your typing. What steps do you take to diagnose the problem?

Skill level: High

Expected answer:

The first step is to determine what is taking all of the system resources. Is a process consuming all of the CPU? Run the 'top' command to see if any processes are consuming the CPU cycles. Also check the load average with 'uptime' to see if the problem existed previously and just went away.

If no CPU load is evident, check the memory usage. Again, the 'top' command will display current memory and swap space in use. If all of the main memory is in use, and the system has to swap to disk for every new process, the response will decrease dramatically.

The final thing to check is disk usage. The 'vmstat' or 'sar -g' commands will display the disk usage. High page-out values mean the system is swapping because of low memory. High disk activity without paging is a sign of some processes doing extensive disk reads or writes.

This situation brings up an important point: it is impossible to know when a system is misbehaving if you don't know what it looks like when it is behaving. Establishing a system benchmark is critical to performance troubleshooting. It could be as simple as knowing what processes should show up in a 'ps -aef' output. A good system administrator will be able to answer these questions about his systems:

- What is the average number of running processes?

- What is the average number of users?

- What is the average CPU load?

- What is the average memory and swap usage?

- What is the average disk usage?

Without this information, diagnosing a problem situation becomes very difficult. There are many good monitoring tools available that can help in tracking this information. Of course, the standard UNIX monitoring tools run from a cron job can provide this information as well.

Score: _____

Comment: _____

_____

Non-Technical Questions

When conducting an on-site or telephone interview, it's very important that you be able to assess non-technical information about your job candidate. These non-technical factors include motivation, thinking skills, and personal attitude. All of these factors have a direct bearing on the ultimate success of the candidate in your shop, and also give you an idea about the longevity of a particular client.

Each of these questions is deliberately ambiguous and probing so that the job candidate will have an opportunity to speak freely. Often these questions will give you a very good idea of the suitability of the candidate for the position. Remember, in many IT shops technical ability is secondary to the ability of the candidate to function as a team member within the organization.

1. What are your plans if you don't get this job?

    This question can reveal a great deal about the motivation of the job candidate. If the candidate indicates that he/she will change career fields, going into an unrelated position, then this person may not have a long-term motivation to stay within the IT industry. If, on the other hand, the candidate responds that he will continue to pursue opportunities within the specific technical area, then the candidate is probably dedicated to the job for which he is being interviewed.

2. How do you feel about overtime?

    This is an especially loaded question, because any honest job candidate is going to tell you that they don't like to work overtime. As we know, the reality of today's IT world is that the professional will occasionally have to work evenings and weekends. This question is essential if you're interviewing for a position that requires non-traditional hours, such as a network administrator or database administrator, where the bulk of the production changes will occur on evenings, weekends, and holidays.

3. Describe your biggest non-technical flaw.

    This question provides insight into the personality of the job candidate, as well as their honesty and candor. Responses are unpredictable and may range from "I don't suffer fools gladly" to "I have a hard time thinking after I've been on the job for 16 hours". Again, there is no right or wrong answer to this question, but it may indicate how well the candidate is going to function during critical moments. More importantly, this question gives an idea of the level of self-awareness of the candidate, and gauges whether or not they are actively working to improve their non-technical skills.

4. Describe your least favorite boss or professor.

    The answer to this question will reveal the candidate's opinions and attitudes about being supervised by others. While there is no correct response to this question, it can shed a great deal of light on the candidate's interpersonal skills.

5. Where do you plan to be ten years from now?

    This is an especially important question for the IT job candidate because it reveals a lot about their motivations. As we know, the IT job industry does not have a lot of room for advancement within the technical arena, and someone who plans to rise within the IT organization will be required to move into management at some point. It's interesting that the response to this question is often made to be overly important, especially amongst those managers that hear the response "in ten years I would like to have your job."

6. How important is money to you?

    Again, this is an extremely misleading question, because even though many IT professionals deeply enjoy their jobs, and some would even do it for free, money is a primary motivator for people in the workplace. This question provides an easy opportunity to find out whether or not your candidate is being honest with you.

    An appropriate answer for the candidate might be to say that he greatly enjoys his work within IT but that he needs to be able to maintain some level of income in order to support his family. A bonus benefit of this question is it also provides insight into the demographic structure of the job candidate, namely their marital status, as well as the age of their children, and whether or not they have immediate family in the area. It's well-known within the IT industry that job candidates are most likely to remain with the company if they have a large extended family group within the immediate area.

7. Why did you leave your last job?

    This is one of the most loaded questions of all, and one that can be extremely revealing about the personality of the IT job candidate. The most appropriate answer to this question is that the previous job was not technically challenging enough, or that the candidate was bored.

    However, periodically you will find job candidates who will express negativity regarding the work environment, the quality of the management, and the personalities of the co-workers. This of course, should be a major red flag, because it may indicate that this job candidate does not possess the interpersonal skills required to succeed in a team environment.

8. If you were a vegetable, what vegetable would you be?

On its face, this is a totally ludicrous and ambiguous question, but it gives you an opportunity to assess the creative thinking skills of the job candidate. For example, if the job candidate merely replies "I don't know," he may not possess the necessary creative thinking skills required for a systems analyst or developer position.

A creative candidate will simply pick a vegetable, and describe in detail why that particular vegetable suits their personality. For example, the job candidate might say "I would be broccoli because I am health-oriented, have a bushy head, and go well with Chinese food".

9. Describe the month of June.

The answer to this question also provides insight into the thinking ability of the job candidate. For example, most job candidates may reply that June is a summer month, with longer days, hot weather, and an ideal vacation time. The candidate with an engineering or scientific point of view might reply instead that June is a month with 30 days, immediately preceding the summer equinox.

10. Why do you want to work here?

This is the candidate's opportunity to express why he might be a good fit for your particular organization. It also indicates whether the candidate has taken the time to research the company and the work environment. Is the candidate applying for this position solely because he needs a job, any job, or because he has specifically singled out your company due to some appealing characteristic of the work environment?

This question can also add information about the motivation of the job candidate, because a job candidate who is highly motivated to work for a particular firm will make the effort to research the company, the work environment, and even the backgrounds of individual managers.

Using a powerful search engine such as Google, the savvy IT candidate can quickly glean information about the person who is interviewing them. Having detailed knowledge of the organization is a very positive indicator that the candidate has given a lot of thought to the particular position and is evidence of high motivation.

General Questions

1. What do you know about our company?

    Answer: _____

    _____

    Comment: _____

    If the prospective employee has little or no knowledge about the company, then he will also have little idea about how he can benefit the company. A candidate who has not gone to the trouble of researching the organization may be after a job, any job.

    A candidate who has taken the time to explore the company will probably have specific ideas in mind about what he can bring to the organization. The initiative required by the candidate to research the company is a good sign that he is proactive and not passive dead weight.

    If the candidate has some knowledge of the company's mission and function, this will also become apparent in the questions he asks you. He will already be thinking about how he can fit in and how his skills can be utilized, desirable traits of the problem-solver.

2. Why do you want to work for this company? Why should we hire you?

    Answer: _____

    _____

    Comment: _____

    The answer to this question can reveal whether the candidate is merely shopping for a job or has true interest in the company and the position. It is important that the candidate show some passion for the field, if he does not, he will probably never be creative in the work environment, and he will not represent a solution for you.

Does the candidate have a core belief that his particular set of skills can benefit you? Answers such as "I believe my experience can make a difference here," or "I believe your company will provide an environment that more directly engages my interest," or "Working for your company will provide challenges that excite me" are good starters.

3. Why are you looking for a new job?

    Answer: _____

    _____

    Comment: _____

Typical reasons for seeking a new job include the desire to advance in the field and boredom in a job that offers few fresh challenges. These are positive motivations, but there can be negative ones as well. There may be personal conflicts between the candidate and other team members or management that have become so adversarial that the candidate is compelled to leave.

While not necessarily eliminating a candidate from consideration, personal friction in the previous job does raise a red flag. It may be that the candidate is an unfortunate victim of backroom politics, but if he confides in you about the shortcomings of his supervisors or fellow employees, while taking no responsibility himself, you must consider yourself warned.

4. Tell us about yourself/your background.

Answer: _____
_____

Comment: _____

This is probably asked more than any other question in interviews. It is the main opportunity for the candidate to describe his experiences, motivations, and vision of himself as it relates to the company.

The candidate should provide clear examples of how his abilities were used in the past to solve problems. If the candidate just repeats the information in the resume, he is probably only going through the motions and has no clear vision of his role in the company. Even worse, if the candidate contradicts the resume, there is evidence of a serious problem.

5. What are the three major characteristics that you bring to the job?

Answer: _____
_____

Comment: _____

The candidate should offer specific skills or traits that he believes will be useful in the position. If the candidate is unable to relate these characteristics to the job, he has obviously not thought much about his role in the organization. You are interested in finding someone who has ideas about how he can hit the ground running and make a real difference to the company.

6. Describe the "ideal" job... the "ideal" supervisor.

Answer: _____

_____

Comment: _____

This question is not as open-ended as it may seem. If the candidate's ideal job has little or nothing in common with the position he is interviewing for, he is unlikely to be a good fit. The candidate's response should match fairly well with the requirements of the position.

The candidate's description of the ideal supervisor can provide clues about how well the candidate works with superiors. Beware of the candidate who seizes this as an opportunity to denigrate past managers.

7. How would you handle a tough customer?

Answer: _____

_____

Comment: _____

Can the candidate provide examples of instances when difficult clients were won over? An effective communicator can strike a balance between meeting the needs of the customer and dealing with unrealistic expectations.

Above all, the candidate should indicate that he understands the necessity of "going the extra mile" to alleviate the concerns of the customer. Providing service to the client or end user is fundamental to the success of any enterprise.

8. How would you handle working with a difficult co-worker?

Answer: _____

_____

Comment: _____

This is similar to the last question. The candidate should relate an example of a conflict with a co-worker or team member that was successfully resolved. What you are looking for is evidence that the candidate is able to facilitate communication and lead a difficult project to a successful conclusion.

9. When would you be available to start if you were selected?

Answer: _____

_____

Comment: _____

10. How does this position match your career goals?

Answer: _____

_____

Comment: _____

This is an excellent question to ascertain whether the candidate truly sees the position as an integral part of his career path. Does the candidate believe the knowledge and experience he will gain from this job will move him to where he wants to be?

A thorough answer to this question will lead into the next one.

11. What are your career goals (a) 3 years from now; (b) 10 years from now?

Answer: _____

_____

Comment: _____

The answer to this question will indicate the level of commitment the candidate feels towards the job and the company. If the candidate has a goal in mind, how well does it fit with the job he is applying for?

When the candidate describes his goals, does he speak in terms of the skills and abilities he hopes to acquire that will prepare him for his eventual role, or does he simply want to be the CEO, with little thought of what it might take to get there?

The interviewer may be surprised by how often the candidate will talk about goals that are unrelated to the position.

12. What do you like to do in your spare time?

Answer: _____

_____

Comment: _____

This question provides an opportunity to learn more about the character of the candidate, and to judge whether his outside interests complement his professional life. Is the candidate well-rounded or one-dimensional? Does he tend to sustain an interest over time?

13. What motivates you to do a good job?

Answer: _____

_____

Comment: _____

If the candidate responds "making money" or "avoiding the wrath of my boss," you probably have a problem. The candidate should describe some positive motivation, such as a new challenge, and tie it to a specific example of a time in the past when the motivation reaped personal rewards and results on the job.

14. What two or three things are most important to you at work?

Answer: _____

_____

Comment: _____

The answer to this can reveal much about how the candidate sees himself on the job. Does the candidate mention things such as the importance of interpersonal communication, or responding quickly to crisis situations, things that facilitate job performance, or does he seem to be more worried about the timeliness of his coffee breaks?

15. What qualities do you think are essential to be successful in this kind of work?

Answer: _____

_____

Comment: _____

Does the candidate have a realistic idea of what the work environment requires of him, and do the qualities of the candidate match the job? Does the candidate have an example of a past job experience when these qualities were called upon with beneficial results?

16. How does your previous work experience prepare you for this position?

Answer: _____

_____

Comment: _____

This question relates to many of the others. If the candidate is able to articulate a clear idea of how his previous experience and training has prepared him for the responsibilities of the new position, he will be well ahead of many other interviewees.

17. How do you define "success"?

Answer: _____

_____

Comment: _____

If the answer doesn't fit the position, the candidate may be unhappy in the field, or quickly become bored. This indicates that the candidate may not be committed to staying with the company for very long.

18. What has been your most significant accomplishment to date?

Answer: _____

_____

Comment: _____

The candidate should be able to relate a specific example of an achievement that demonstrates a desirable quality for the job. The candidate should focus on action and results, rather than long-winded descriptions of situations.

The answer to this question can provide insight into situations that the candidate may handle especially well. The candidate should demonstrate an ability to persevere and overcome obstacles. Did the person deliver more than was expected of him in a difficult situation?

19. Describe a failure and how you dealt with it.

Answer: _____

_____

Comment: _____

This is known as a negative question, and it can be extremely revealing. It can indicate significant weaknesses or problems that may interfere with the ability to do the job.

Was the failure a catastrophic one, or a relatively minor problem? Was the candidate able to learn from the experience and apply the knowledge to future situations?

The answer to this question can also reveal how much personal accountability and responsibility the candidate accepts. If the candidate blames the failure on others, he is not likely to learn from his mistakes.

As with most interview questions, this question is designed to provide insight into the overall personality of the candidate, and gives you a fuller appreciation of the strengths, as well as the weaknesses, of the person.

20. What leadership roles have you held?

Answer: _____

_____

Comment: _____

This answer should indicate not only that the candidate has the leadership experience to succeed in the new job, but that he has the ability to work well with others and is able to shoulder the responsibility and deal with the pressure associated with the requirements of the position.

21. Are you willing to travel?

Answer: _____

_____

Comment: _____

The answer here will demonstrate how committed to the company the candidate is likely to be. If the candidate dismisses the idea of travel completely, he may lack the motivation you are looking for.

22. What have you done in the past year to improve yourself?

Answer: _____

_____

Comment: _____

This question can shed more light on the personality of the candidate. If the candidate has been motivated by the goal of obtaining this position, he will be able to demonstrate that he has taken the initiative to prepare himself for it.

If the candidate instead chooses to describe the benefits of his basket-weaving class, he may indeed be the better for it, but it has little relevance to solving the problems he would soon encounter in the new position.

23. In what areas do you feel you need further education and training to be successful?

Answer: _____

_____

Comment: _____

If the answer has nothing to do with the offered position, the candidate may soon become bored. This question is similar to others and should dovetail with other answers about goals and career path.

24. What are your salary requirements?

Answer: _____

_____

Comment: _____

If the candidate mentions a figure that is too low, he may be uninformed or desperate. On the other hand, if his financial expectations are unreasonable, he should probably be eliminated from consideration.

The following questions are designed to zero in on key aspects of the candidate's personality and ability to perform. You may find it helpful to assign each response a score between 1 and 5 (a shorthand assessment technique that may also be used with many of the preceding questions).

Policies, Processes and Procedures

Able to act in accordance with established guidelines, follow standard procedures in crisis situations, communicate and enforce organizational policies and procedures, recognize and constructively conform to unwritten rules or practices.

1. On some jobs it is necessary to act strictly in accordance with policy. Give me an example when you were expected to act in accordance with policy even when it was not convenient. What did you do?

    Expected answer: Did the candidate follow policy because of commitment to it, even if a reason could be given for breaking it? Was there non-conformity to policy because of personal style, disrespect for those who made the policy, or revenge/dishonesty?

    Score: _____

    Comment: _____

    _____

2. What types of experience have you had in managing situations that involve potentially high money loss situations to ensure your job effectiveness?

    Expected answer: Did the candidate have a "no exceptions" strategy which showed systematic and rigorous use of policy and procedures to ensure consistency? Was there a dislike for rules and preferences to ensure consistency? Was there dislike for rules and preference for doing the job his/her own way?

Score: _____

Comment: _____

_____

3. Describe a time when you found a policy or procedure
   challenging or difficult to adhere to. How did you handle it?

   Expected answer: Did the candidate take great pains to
   adhere to the policy and communicate the difficulty to
   proper management for review/revision? Was there an
   unnecessary risky deviation from policy, and no
   communication of either the challenge or deviation to
   management?

   Score: _____

   Comment: _____

   _____

Quality

Ability to maintain high standards despite pressing deadlines, establish high standards and measures, do work right the first time and inspect material for flaws, test new methods thoroughly, reinforce excellence as a fundamental priority.

1. Describe a situation in which a crucial deadline was nearing, but you didn't want to compromise quality. How did you deal with it?

    Expected answer: Did the candidate maintain high quality through investing additional resources, moving deadlines, or making a statement of work in progress? Was there a quality sacrifice, possibly resulting in additional problems at a later time?

    Score: _____

    Comment: _____

    _____

2. Describe something you developed or coordinated that had to be exactly right. Exactly how did you test it?

    Expected answer: Did the candidate rigorously identify potential sources of problems and systematically address those, and run ample trails? Was there a brief accounting for possible problems, insufficient experimentation, or minimal piloting?

    Score: _____

    Comment: _____

    _____

3. Describe an effort you undertook to make product/service quality a fundamental priority in your business. Exactly what steps did you take to do this?

> **Expected answer**: Did the candidate implement training and error prevention/control/correction systems, or apply other systematic approaches? Was there a haphazard or inadequate support of quality functions?

Score: _____

Comment: _____

_____

Commitment to Task

Ability to take responsibility for actions and outcomes and persist despite obstacles, be available around the clock in case of emergency; give long hours to the job; demonstrate dependability in difficult circumstances and show a sense of urgency about getting the job done.

1. Describe a difficult situation in which you took full responsibility for actions and outcomes. How did you act on this?

    Expected answer: Did the candidate publicly claim responsibility, and then carefully manage this situation to success, possibly one involving other parties with divergent goals? Was there allowance of others to accept blame, and little effort to resolve a difficult situation?

    Score: _____

    Comment: _____

    _____

2. Some people can be counted on to go the extra mile when their organization really needs it. Describe a time when you demonstrated dependability in trying circumstances.

    Expected answer: Did the candidate work long hours or perform unusual job duties to help the organization get through a personnel shortage, unusual time demands, etc.? Was there minimal extra effort, consistent with the notion that it was the company's problem?

    Score: _____

    Comment: _____

    _____

3. Describe a time when you gave long hours to the job. For example, tell me about when you took work home, worked on weekends, or maintained long hours due to system maintenance.

> Expected answer: Did the candidate show self-direction and initiative in working particularly long hours, with clear dedication to a meaningful objective? Was there compliance to routine work requirements, possibly with resentment about what was expected?

Score: _____

Comment: _____

_____

4. Give me an example of a time when you demonstrated a sense of urgency about getting results.

> **Expected answer**: Did the candidate take immediate action directed toward a specific objective, so that non-task activities and interests were given low priority while productivity and efficiency were of prime importance? Was there little emphasis on effectiveness/speed/efficiency?

Score: _____

Comment: _____

_____

Planning, Prioritizing and Goal Setting

Ability to prepare for emerging customer needs; manage multiple projects; determine project urgency in a meaningful and practical way; use goals to guide actions and create detailed action plans; organize and schedule people and tasks.

1. Describe a situation that illustrates how well you manage multiple projects at one time.

   Expected answer: Did the candidate keep all projects moving on a pace to hit deadlines and in a manageable, systematic, quality way, and using a meaningful approach to prioritizing? Was there haphazard allotment of resources to different tasks, with unproductive and unnecessary chaos?

   Score: _____

   Comment: _____

   _____

2. Priorities can be set meaningfully based on ease of task, customer size, deadlines, or a number of other factors. Describe a time when it was challenging for you to prioritize.

   Expected answer: Did the candidate use a sensible set or priorities and apply it consistently? Was there excess bouncing of resources, resulting in inefficiency, or a poor choice of criteria on which to prioritize?

   Score: _____

   Comment: _____

   _____

3. Think of a project in which you skillfully coordinated people, tasks, and schedules. How did you do it?

> Expected answer: Did the candidate use a systematic approach to identify tasks, people who can do the tasks, schedules, and constraints? Was there a simplistic approach that was inadequate given the complexities of the project?

Score: _____

Comment: _____

_____

Attention to Detail

Ability to be alert in a high-risk environment; follow detailed procedures and ensure accuracy in documentation and data; carefully monitor gauges, instruments, or processes; concentrate on routine work details and organize and maintain a system of records.

1. Describe a time when you had to apply changes to a mission critical system. What did you do to insure the stability of the system? What actions did you take and what were the results?

   Expected answer: Did the candidate dutifully monitor all potentially troublesome aspects of the environment, and address anything that seemed imperfect. Was there a casual awareness of potential trouble spots, and reliance on subsequent quick reactions rather than prevention?

   Score: _____

   Comment: _____

   _____

2. Select an experience from your past, which illustrates your ability to be attentive to detail when monitoring the systems environment. Tell me, in detail, what happened.

   Expected answer: Did the candidate show commitment to monitoring and understanding equipment and to using a strategy to ensure/enhance attention to detail? Was there little awareness of potential distractions, over-dependence on technology, or overconfidence?

   Score: _____

   Comment: _____

   _____

3. How have you gone about ensuring accuracy and consistency in a document or data you were preparing? Tell me about a specific case in which your attention to detail paid off.

   Expected answer: Did the candidate take clear precautions such as proofing thoroughly, double-checking, verifying format consistency, etc.? Was there only a cursory spot check?

   Score: _____

   Comment: _____

   _____

4. Tell me about your experience in dealing with routine work. What kinds of problems did you have to overcome in order to concentrate on the details of the job?

   Expected answer: Did the candidate use a strategy to maintain attentiveness during routine work? Was there acceptance of diminished alertness, with little effort being made to remove/reduce it?

   Score: _____

   Comment: _____

   _____

5. Give me an example that demonstrates your ability to organize and maintain a system of records.

   Expected answer: Did the candidate initiate or show commitment to a systematic method for organization or record keeping? Was there ineffective record keeping, overconfidence in memory, or dependence on others?

Score: _____

Comment: _____

_____

Initiative

Ability to bring about great results from ordinary circumstances; prepare for problems or opportunities in advance; transform leads into productive business outcomes; undertake additional responsibilities and respond to situations as they arise without supervision.

1. Tell me about a situation in which you aggressively capitalized on an opportunity and converted something ordinary into something special.

    Expected answer: Did the candidate put a unique twist on a routine situation to yield unusually positive results, probably not achieved by others in similar situations? Was there an accomplishment of little magnitude or that should have been expected of anyone in that situation?

    Score: _____

    Comment: _____

    _____

2. Describe something you've done that shows how you can respond to situations as they arise without supervision.

    Expected answer: Did the candidate take reasonable and quick action with an appropriate amount of information or research, warranting the independence? Was there use of authority inappropriately, excess procrastination, or a bad decision?

    Score: _____

    Comment: _____

    _____

3. Describe a time when you voluntarily undertook a special project above and beyond your normal responsibilities.

Expected answer: Did the candidate volunteer for a large task/responsibility despite an already full workload and succeed without undue compromise or other responsibilities? Was there an insignificant, short-term addition, or an unnecessary sacrifice of other areas?

Score: _____

Comment: _____

_____

4. Many people have good ideas, but few act on them. Tell me how you've transformed a good idea into a productive business outcome.

Expected answer: Did the candidate generate a meaningful action plan to bring the idea to reality? Was there a haphazard, unrealistic, unproductive transformation?

Score: _____

Comment: _____

_____

Index

About Adam Haeder

Adam Haeder is one of the nation's foremost experts in Network Administration and Linux technology. A respected instructor and brilliant author, Adam is a Vice President at the prestigious Applied Information Management Institute in Omaha, Nebraska. Expert in Intel hardware and Network Administrator internals, Adam possesses the rare combination of management and technical expertise that is critical to an outstanding IT consultant. Adam is a Linux Certified Administrator (LCA), a Cisco Certified Networking Associate (CCNA), and a Cisco Certified Academic Instructor (CCAI).

About Mike Reed

When he first started drawing, Mike Reed drew just to amuse himself. It wasn't long, though, before he knew he wanted to be an artist.

Today he does illustrations for children's books, magazines, catalogs, and ads.

He also teaches illustration at the College of Visual Art in St. Paul, Minnesota. Mike Reed says, "Making pictures is like acting — you can paint yourself into the action." He often paints on the computer, but he also draws in pen and ink and paints in acrylics. He feels that learning to draw well is the key to being a successful artist.

Mike is regarded as one of the nation's premier illustrators and is the creator of the popular "Flame Warriors" illustrations at **www.flamewarriors.com**. A renowned children's artist, Mike has also provided the illustrations for dozens of children's books.

Mike Reed has always enjoyed reading. As a young child, he liked the Dr. Seuss books. Later, he started reading biographies and war stories. One reason why he feels lucky to be an illustrator is because he can listen to books on tape while he works. Mike is available to provide custom illustrations for all manner of publications at reasonable prices. Mike can be reached at **www.mikereedillustration.com**.

Conducting the Oracle Job Interview

IT Manager's Guide for Oracle Job Interviews with Oracle Interview Questions

Mike Ault & Don Burleson

ISBN 0-9727513-1-9

Retail Price $16.95 / £10.95

As professional consultants, Don Burleson and Mike Ault have interviewed hundreds of Oracle job candidates. With over four decades of interviewing experience, Ault and Burleson tell you how to quickly identify acceptable Oracle job candidates by asking the right Oracle job interview questions.

Mike Ault and Don Burleson are recognized as the two best-selling Oracle Authors in the world. With combined authorship of over 25 books, Ault & Burleson are the two most respected Oracle authorities on the planet. For the first time ever, Ault & Burleson combine their talents in this exceptional handbook.

Using Oracle job interview questions that are not available to the general public, the IT manager will be able to quickly access the technical ability of any Oracle job candidate. In today's market, there are thousands of under-trained Oracle professionals, and the IT manager must be able to quickly access the true ability of the Oracle job candidate.

www.Rampant-Books.com

Conducting the Network Administrator Job Interview

IT Manager Guide with Cisco CCNA Interview Questions

Adam Haeder

ISBN 0-9744355-7-0

Retail Price $16.95 / £10.95

This book is the accumulated observations of the authors' interviews with hundreds of job candidates. The author provides useful insights into what characteristics make a good Network Administrator programmer and offer their accumulated techniques as an aid to interviewing an Network Administrator job candidate.

This handy guide has a complete set of Network Administrator job interview questions and provides a complete method for accurately accessing the technical abilities of Network Administrator job candidates. By using Network Administrator job interview questions that only an experienced person knows, your supervisor can ask the right interview questions and fill your Network Administrator job with the best qualified Network Administrator developer.

www.Rampant-Books.com

Conducting the Web Master Job Interview

IT Manager Guide with Interview Questions

Janet Burleson

ISBN 0-9745993-1-X

Retail Price $16.95 / £10.95

As a professional web master, Janet Burleson has extensive experience interviewing web master job candidates. With over a decade of interviewing experience, Burleson tell you how to quickly identify acceptable web master job candidates by asking the right web master job interview questions.

This book is the accumulated observations of the author's interviews with hundreds of job candidates. The author provides useful insights into what characteristics make a good web master programmer and offers her accumulated techniques as an aid to interviewing a web master job candidate.

This handy guide has a complete set of web master job interview questions and provides a complete method for accurately assessing the technical abilities of web master job candidates. By using web master job interview questions that only an experienced person knows, your supervisor can ask the right interview questions and fill your web master job with the best qualified web master developer.

www.Rampant-Books.com

The Oracle In-Focus Series

The *Oracle In-Focus* series is a unique publishing paradigm, targeted at Oracle professionals who need fast and accurate working examples of complex issues. *Oracle In-Focus* books are unique because they have a super-tight focus and quickly provide Oracle professionals with what they need to solve their problems.

Oracle In-Focus books are designed for the practicing Oracle professional. Oracle In-Focus books are an affordable way for all Oracle professionals to get the information they need, and get it fast.

Expert Authors – All *Oracle In-Focus* authors are content experts and are carefully screened for technical ability and communications skills.

Online Code Depot – All code scripts from *Oracle In-Focus* are available on the web for instant download. Those who purchase a book will get the URL and password to download their scripts.

Lots of working examples – *Oracle In-Focus* is packed with working examples and pragmatic tips.

No theory – Practicing Oracle professionals know the concepts, they need working code to get started fast.

Concise – All *Oracle In-Focus* books are less than 200 pages and get right to-the-point of the tough technical issues.

Tight focus - The *Oracle In-Focus* series addresses tight topics and targets specific technical areas of Oracle technology.

Affordable – Reasonably priced, *Oracle In-Focus* books are the perfect solution to challenging technical issues.

www.Rampant-Books.com

Free!
Oracle 10g Senior DBA Reference Poster

This 24 x 36 inch quick reference includes the important data columns and relationships between the DBA views, allowing you to quickly write complex data dictionary queries.

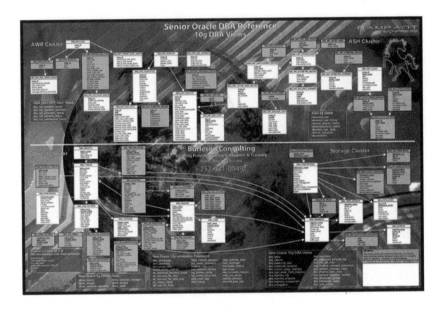

This comprehensive data dictionary reference contains the most important columns from the most important Oracle10g DBA views. Especially useful are the Automated Workload Repository (AWR) and Active Session History (ASH) DBA views.

WARNING - This poster is not suitable for beginners. It is designed for senior Oracle DBAs and requires knowledge of Oracle data dictionary internal structures. You can get your poster at this URL:

www.rampant.cc/poster.htm